W9-AFS-039

The Land and People of

MONGOLIA

PORTRAITS OF THE NATIONS

The Land and People of ®
MONGOLIA

by John S. Major

J. B. LIPPINCOTT   NEW YORK

Country maps by Joe LeMonnier

Every effort has been made to locate the copyright holders
of all copyrighted photographs and to secure the necessary
permission to reproduce them. In the event of any questions
arising as to their use, the publisher will be glad to make
necessary changes in future printings and editions.
All photos not credited are courtesy of John S. Major

The quote on page 45 is from Otto J. Maenchen-Helfen,
The World of the Huns (Berkeley and Los Angeles:
University of California Press, 1973), p. 206.

THE LAND AND PEOPLE OF
is a registered trademark of
Harper & Row, Publishers, Inc.

The Land and People of Mongolia
Copyright © 1990 by John S. Major
Printed in the U.S.A. All rights reserved.
For information address J. B. Lippincott Junior Books,
10 East 53rd Street, New York, N.Y. 10022
10 9 8 7 6 5 4 3 2 1
First Edition

Library of Congress Cataloging-in-Publication Data
Major, John S.
   The land and people of Mongolia / John Major.
      p.   cm. — (Portraits of the nations series)
   Includes bibliographical references.
   Summary: Introduces the history, geography, people, culture,
government, and economy of Mongolia.
   ISBN 0-397-32386-7 : $. — ISBN 0-397-32387-5 (lib. bdg.) :
$
   1. Mongolia—History—Juvenile literature.   [1. Mongolia.]
I. Title. II. Series.
DS798.5.M35 1990   89-37790
951.73—dc20   CIP
                                                        AC

In Memory of Owen Lattimore

Contents

THE WORLD

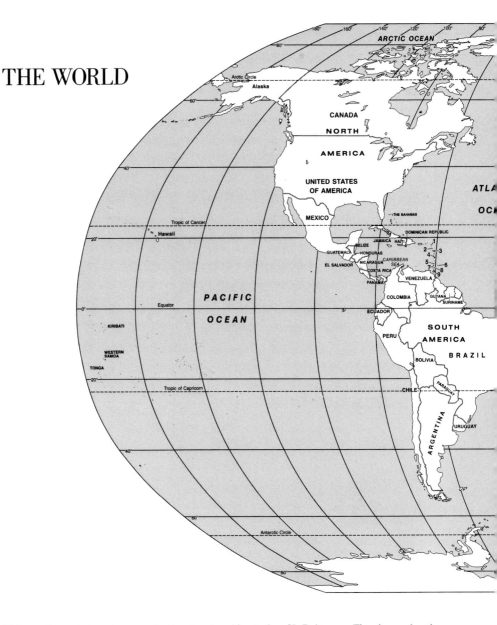

This world map is based on a projection developed by Arthur H. Robinson. The shape of each country and its size, relative to other countries, are more accurately expressed here than in previous maps. The map also gives equal importance to all of the continents, instead of placing North America at the center of the world. *Used by permission of the Foreign Policy Association.*

Legend

——— International boundaries

--------- Disputed or undefined boundaries

Projection: Robinson

| 0 | 1000 | 2000 | 3000 Miles |

| 0 | 1000 | 2000 | 3000 Kilometers |

Caribbean Nations

1. Anguilla
2. St. Christopher and Nevis
3. Antigua and Barbuda
4. Dominica
5. St. Lucia
6. Barbados
7. St. Vincent
8. Grenada
9. Trinidad and Tobago

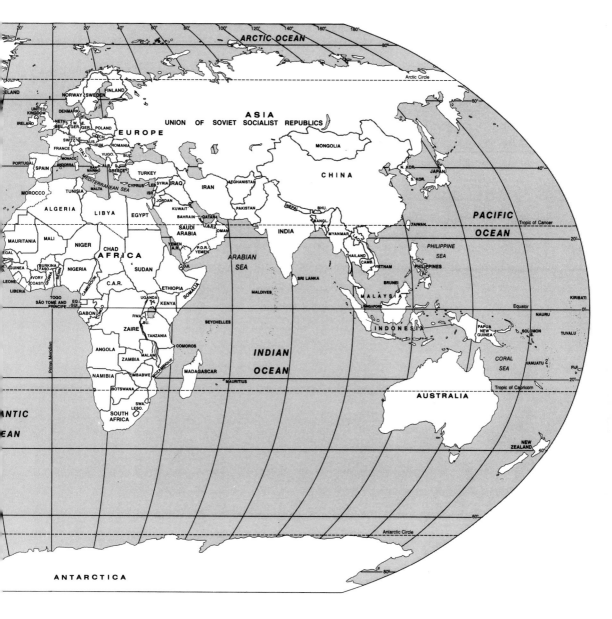

Abbreviations

ALB.	—Albania	C.A.R.	—Central African Republic	LEB.	—Lebanon	RWA.	—Rwanda
AUS.	—Austria	CZECH.	—Czechoslovakia	LESO.	—Lesotho	S. KOR.	—South Korea
BANGL.	—Bangladesh	DJI.	—Djibouti	LIE.	—Liechtenstein	SWA.	—Swaziland
BEL.	—Belgium	E.GER.	—East Germany	LUX.	—Luxemburg	SWITZ.	—Switzerland
BHU.	—Bhutan	EQ. GUI.	—Equatorial Guinea	NETH.	—Netherlands	U.A.E.	—United Arab Emirates
BU.	—Burundi	GUI. BIS.	—Guinea Bissau	N. KOR.	—North Korea	W. GER.	—West Germany
BUL.	—Bulgaria	HUN.	—Hungary	P.D.R.–YEMEN	—People's Democratic	YEMEN A.R.	—Yemen Arab Republic
CAMB.	—Cambodia	ISR.	—Israel		Republic of Yemen	YUGO.	—Yugoslavia

Mini Facts

OFFICIAL NAME: Mongolian People's Republic

LOCATION: Eastern Central Asia, south of Siberia and north of China. Borders with the Soviet Union on the north and the People's Republic of China on the south.

AREA: 604,100 square miles (1,566,500 square kilometers)

CAPITAL: Ulan Bator (official spelling: Ulaanbaatar)

POPULATION: 1,940,000 (1987 est.): cities and towns, 51%; rural 49%

MAJOR LANGUAGE: Khalka Mongolian

RELIGIONS: Officially atheistic. Lamaistic Buddhism and Islam continue to be practiced but no longer play a major role in society.

TYPE OF GOVERNMENT: Socialist Republic

HEAD OF STATE: President

HEAD OF GOVERNMENT: Premier

HEAD OF PARTY: General Secretary

PARLIAMENT: People's Great Khural (elected every four years) enacts laws; Mongolian People's Revolutionary Party sets policy

ADMINISTRATIVE SUBDIVISIONS: 18 provinces (*aimags*), 3 autonomous cities

ADULT LITERACY: 80% (1986 est.)

LIFE EXPECTANCY: Female, 66.8; Male, 62.9 (1986 est.)

MAIN PRODUCTS: *Herding and agriculture*—livestock (sheep, goats, horses, camels, and others) and animal products, including meat, dairy products, hides, and wool; grain (wheat, oats, barley); animal fodder; potatoes and vegetables. Fur trapping is commercially important
Manufacturing and processing—food processing, leather and leather goods, textiles, chemicals, cement
Mining—Coal, copper, molybdenum, phosphates, tin, nickel, zinc, tungsten, fluorspar, gold

CURRENCY: Tugrik

A Note on the
Spelling of Mongolian Words

There is no single, generally accepted system for transposing the spelling of Mongolian words from Mongolian or Cyrillic script to the letters of the Roman alphabet. Scholarly works by specialists in Mongolian studies employ a system that is highly accurate but (because it uses special letters and diacritical marks) is generally unintelligible to the untrained reader. Popular works on Mongolia use a great variety of systems, so that, for example, the name Genghis Khan might also be rendered Genghiz, Jenghis, Chinggis, and so on. Many authors replace "Kh" with "H," so that, for example, the Khangai Region becomes the Hangai Region.

In this book, we have tried to adhere to a simple utilitarian principal: Mongolian names are given in the forms in which they are most likely to be encountered in other works—especially reference works—on Mongolia, and which, when pronounced by an ordinary reader of English, will yield a reasonable approximation of the sound of spoken Mongolian. For geographical names, we follow the usage of *The New York Times Atlas of the World,* except in a few instances where the atlas spelling has been altered to conform to the spelling used elsewhere in this book (for example, Altai and Choibalsan).

Who Are the Mongols?

Genghis Khan is one of the most famous people in history. For most of the world, his name calls to mind images of wild horsemen sweeping across the plains of Asia, attacking towns and cities, slaughtering the inhabitants, and riding off with as much loot as they could carry. In the West, if we use the word "Mongol" at all it is often in the phrase "Mongol hordes," a kind of shorthand for the idea of savage, bloodthirsty conquest.

Genghis Khan was indeed a ruthless warrior, a brilliant battlefield commander, a man whose vision of conquest embraced the whole world as he knew it. He inspired his followers and terrified his enemies. He was capable of butchering the entire populations of cities that resisted his conquering armies, yet he could send beggars away from his tent laden with bags of gold. He conquered more territory than anyone else in history, and imposed his personality on the world.

For the Mongol people, Genghis Khan is a national hero, a leader who almost single-handedly made the Mongols the rulers of most of Asia and Eastern Europe. More than that, he was the founder of a nation and the creator of a people. Genghis Khan's first achievement was to unite the scattered tribes of the Mongolian steppes—the grasslands and deserts between China and Siberia—and turn them into Mongols. For a brief time, in the early thirteenth century, he led the Mongols from their homeland deep within the Asian continent to a position of wealth, power, and fame, and thus won them a permanent place in world history.

Genghis Khan united the tribes by warfare, but he ruled them through law. His code of law, the *yasa*, set the standards forever after for the people of the steppe, people who traveled, hunted, and fought

The Yasa

No written copy of the *yasa* law code survives from the time of Genghis Khan, and it is possible that the laws were never written down during his lifetime. From quotations in other sources, however, we know many of the provisions of Genghis Khan's law.

Much of the law related specifically to the military needs of tribal society. For example, horse theft, running away from the battlefield, and communicating with the enemy without permission were all punishable by death.

Tribal customs were also enforced by the law. Reflecting the basic social equality of tribal life, the ruler was allowed to take no

on horseback, and who lived by tending sheep, camels, and other grazing animals. In announcing his code of laws, Genghis Khan proclaimed that it would apply to all the "people who live in felt tents."

The People of the Felt Tents

The tents Genghis Khan had in mind were the round, easily portable felt dwellings of Central Asian nomads, the kind of tent called *ger* in Mongolian but usually known in the West by its Turkish name, yurt. The people of the felt tents—speaking many different languages, believing in many different religions—could be found all across the steppe belt of Asia, from western Manchuria to the Anatolian Plateau.

The people subject to the Great Khan's law, the nomadic tribespeople of Central Asia, were made hardy and strong by the demands of their harsh lifestyle. They valued, above all, courage, self-reliance, and per-

title other than "khan," ("chief"). On the other hand, the dignity of tribal leaders was upheld by law: It was a crime to step on the threshold of a chief's tent, or to climb on the roof of anyone's tent.

The *yasa* not only dealt with crimes, it also protected individual rights. It prohibited chiefs from seizing the property of other tribesmen without just cause, and it provided that the property of any man who died without an adult male heir should be distributed among his women and children.

The *yasa* was very clearly the product of an arid environment. One of its most curious provisions called for the execution of anyone who polluted drinking water by bathing or washing clothes in it.

The Ger

The *ger*, or round felt tent (usually known in English by its Turkish
name, yurt) has been the standard dwelling of the Mongolian steppe
for at least two thousand years. It is perfectly suited to nomadic life
on the windswept plains, being warm in the winter, well ventilated
in the summer, easy to assemble and disassemble, and readily
portable. An average-sized *ger* weighs about 600 pounds;
disassembled, it can easily be carried in an oxcart or loaded onto a
single pack camel.

The basic structure of the *ger* is provided by collapsible
latticework frames called *khana*. *Khana* are made in standard sizes;
the number used determines the diameter of the *ger*. The *khana* are
lashed together leaving room for a wooden doorframe and door,
and placed around a sectional board floor. In the center of the
circle, the *toono*—a round wooden ceiling support rather like a
spoked wagon wheel—is raised on two wooden pillars. Thin wooden
poles are then placed overhead, connecting the edge of the *toono*
with the top of the *khana* framework. At that point the structure of
the *ger* is complete; it is then covered with large sheets of thick
felt, a sturdy cloth made of matted wool. The felt covering is tied
around the outside of the *khana* and secured overhead by long
ropes. The *toono* is left open for ventilation and to allow smoke to
escape, but may be partly or entirely closed by a moveable felt flap.

Within the *ger*, a square hearth is constructed directly under the
toono (although nowadays the open hearth is often replaced by an
iron stove). Wooden beds and storage chests are placed in a circle
around the inside of the lattice walls. The furniture, doorframe, and
door are richly carved and painted in red and yellow, adding bright

accents to the white or pale-gray felt structure. Traditionally the Mongols thought of the *ger* as a miniature universe, with the domed ceiling representing heaven and the square hearth representing earth. Accordingly, Mongolian etiquette demands that the *ger* be treated with respect; it is regarded as extremely rude to step upon or stumble against the base of the doorframe, or to step into or soil the hearth.

In the nineteenth century, Western explorers in Mongolia often described life in a *ger* as efficient, but not necessarily comfortable. The interior of the *ger* was often smoky from the open hearth, and the smell of butter and roasting meat did nothing to improve the atmosphere. Clothes, sheepskin coats, and bedding were seldom washed because of the arid climate, and so the *ger* was frequently infested with lice and fleas. Life in a tent seemed cramped and crowded to visitors used to large houses.

The *ger* of Mongolia today is far more comfortable. The iron stove has solved the problem of smoke, while improved standards of sanitation have made dirt and vermin less bothersome. In good weather, much of daily life is lived outside the *ger*, under the open sky. The *ger* remains so central to Mongolian life that the capital city of Mongolia, Ulan Bator, is surrounded by large suburbs of tents permanently erected on round wooden floor platforms. Many of them are occupied year-round; others are the summer homes of people who prefer to spend the winter in heated urban apartments. Family life in the small space of a *ger* demands courtesy and consideration, but for many Mongols, the *ger* has stood the test of time; they remain by preference ''people who live in felt tents.''

A modern yurt (ger) *in the Khangai. Note the iron stovepipe emerging from the* toono *and the small tractor and motorcycle parked nearby.*

sonal honor. Men defended the flocks and the grazing lands, hunted, and, when the opportunity presented itself, carried out raids against farmers and town dwellers. Women tended the flocks, took care of the camps, and bore full responsibility for the lives of their families when the men were away hunting or raiding.

Although Genghis Khan applied his law equally to all tent dwellers, he did not consider all tent-dwelling people to be Mongols. The Mongols were his own people, a people created from a few closely related tribes united under his own leadership. Turks and Turkomens, Uighurs and Kazakhs, Tumens and Tibetans, were clearly different peoples, often former enemies turned into allies after they had been crushed by military defeat. But all shared the nomadic life that the Great Khan regarded as the only proper life for free people, and so he extended to

Two Mongol herdsmen on a horse-breeding farm. Although city life and industry are important in Mongolia today, livestock raising is still the most important activity, and half of Mongolia's people still live in the countryside.

them the freedom and the responsibility of his law. Within his empire, town dwellers and farmers, merchants and bureaucrats were subjects of the Khan, to be looted or taxed, enslaved or employed, as the Mongols saw fit.

When the Mongol Empire collapsed, less than two centuries after Genghis Khan's death, the Mongols were absorbed into the local populations of the different parts of the empire, or retreated to their old homeland on the Mongolian steppe. But the principles of the *yasa* left their mark on tribal law all across Asia, wherever people lived in felt tents. As for the Mongols themselves, they never forgot that at one time they were the rulers of most of the world, and they never lost the sense of national identity that was their legacy from Genghis Khan.

Mongolian National Identity

The culture of the Mongols is closely bound up with their traditional lifestyle of herding flocks of animals from place to place. The flocks of sheep and goats, and herds of horses, camels, cattle, and other domestic animals that provide the Mongols with their main livelihood, also provide them with most of the essential elements of their culture.

For example, the typical Mongolian diet is heavily based on meat, and especially on such dairy products as cheese, yoghurt, and fermented milk. Bread, potatoes, and vegetables are eaten, of course, but the basic ingredients of Mongolian cooking come from animals. The flocks and herds also provide the raw materials for textiles and clothing: leather for boots and hats, wool for felt (used to make hats as well as for covering tents) and for woolen cloth, and skins for fleece-lined coats and cloaks.

The entire structure of Mongolian society, and the traditional organization of that society into families, clans, and tribes, reflected the nomadic lifestyle of the people. Control over rights to grazing lands, and the management of people and animals so that annual migrations between summer and winter pastures could be made in safety, dictated both the organization of society and the nature of leadership. The cycle of life revolved around the raising, protection, and marketing of domestic animals. People tended to live in relative isolation for much of every year, coming together in larger groups only for migrations or for great annual fairs at which animals were sold. The need to follow the herds meant that everything that families owned—from tents to furniture—had to be portable.

This "portable culture" has also had a profound effect on the artistic life of the Mongols. Articles of daily use, such as saddles and other horse trappings, carved wooden tent doors, wooden storage chests, and bed frames, and jewelry, knives, and other metal articles were often richly decorated in traditional patterns. Painting and sculpture were confined to use in temples and in the palaces of the small, wealthy upper class—those who could afford to live in one place rather than following the flocks on their migrations.

The most characteristic and highly developed Mongolian arts are those that require little or no equipment: poetry, music, and dance. The chanting or singing of poetry, including long epics about tribal heroes and songs in praise of fine horses and the beauty of the Mongolian land, is a favorite activity in the encampments of Mongolian herders; often the singing is accompanied by flutes, fiddles, and other instruments. Music also accompanies dancing, which is an important part of any Mongolian festival or celebration.

A Mongol caravaneer leading a string of camels into a Chinese town in Inner Mongolia, 1923. Until recent times, almost all trade between Mongolia and China was carried on by caravans like this one. The Peabody Museum, Harvard University. Photograph by F. R. Wulsin. Copyright © 1923 by the President and Fellows of Harvard University.

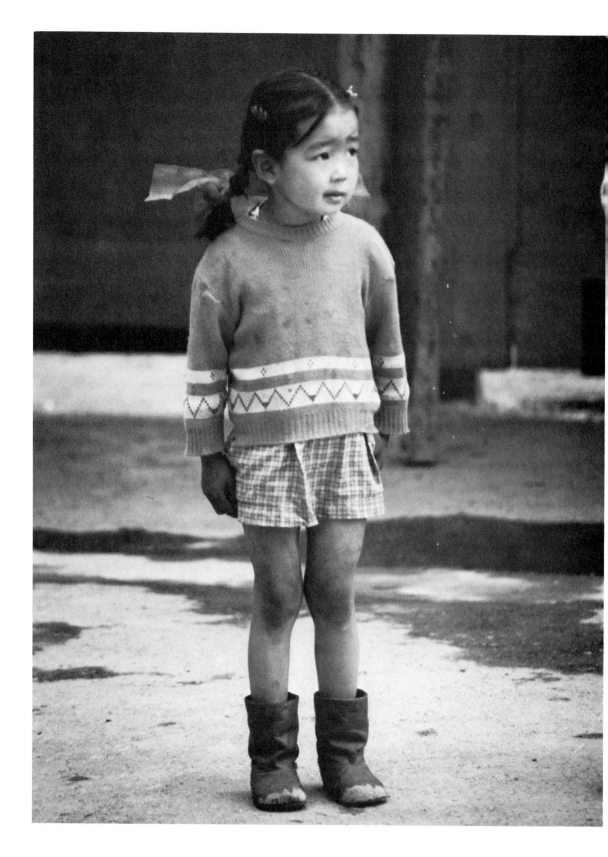

Sports, too, are an essential part of Mongolian culture. Traditionally every Mongolian man was expected to be proficient at the "three manly games," horse racing, archery, and wrestling. Competition in these sports was a part of every festival or celebration on the steppe, and champions won great fame and glory for themselves and their tribe or clan. Even today, when many people in the Mongolian People's Republic live in cities and work at jobs unconnected with livestock, interest and participation in these traditional sports remains nearly universal. Mongolian women are often highly proficient in riding and archery, and festivals include women's events in those sports; by long-standing custom, however, women do not compete in wrestling.

Mongolian national identity is also closely bound up with the mountains, rivers, and vast open steppes of the country itself. The original religion of the Mongols was shamanism, a kind of nature worship in which the sky, the sun and moon, and great mountains and rivers were revered as the homes of gods and goddesses. Although Buddhism became the dominant religion of Mongolia after the fall of the Mongol Empire, and Buddhist temples played an important role in culture and society, this reverence for nature never disappeared. Personal characteristics that were highly valued in Mongolian society, such as cheerfulness in the face of hardship and hospitality to strangers, reflected the life of a people tending their flocks in a huge, sparsely populated, majestic but sometimes dangerous landscape.

Although just over half of the people in the Mongolian People's Republic now live in towns and cities, and many work in mines, factories, and offices, the sense of what it means to be a Mongol continues to be defined to a large degree by a love for the country's land, its poetry

A young girl in Ulan Bator. The Mongolian People's Republic is a young country; half of the population is under twenty-five years of age.

and music, its flocks and felt tents. Mongolian society has been profoundly transformed in the twentieth century by revolution, modernization, and the introduction of a socialist—and often severely repressive—political and economic structure. Nevertheless, Mongolia today continues to be deeply influenced by history and by the ancient culture of the steppes.

The Mongol Tribes

Traditionally, the Mongolian people organized themselves into a fluid and flexible system of confederations, tribes, clans, and families. From the seventeenth to the nineteenth centuries, when Mongolia was ruled by the Qing Dynasty of China, the tribal alignments became more rigid as they were incorporated into a more centralized administrative system imposed by the Chinese. (For more about the Chinese administrative system, see *The Land and People of China.*) Every Mongol was required to belong to a tribe, and the confederations of tribes were made permanent. Each confederation was also assigned to a definite geographical territory. The legacy of that system remains today, as Mongols, both within Mongolia itself and in surrounding territories in China and the Soviet Union, identify themselves with one or another of the old confederations.

In the Mongolian People's Republic, almost 80 percent of the people are Khalkas, direct descendants of the Mongols of the central steppes. Another 5 percent are Turco-Mongolian Kazakhs, 10 percent are members of other Mongol confederations and tribes, and 5 percent are of Russian, Chinese, Manchu, Korean, or other descent. The Khalkas are primarily a people of the grasslands and the green valleys of Mongolia's mountainous regions, horse-riding pastoralists at home on the short-grass prairie of the steppes. Today, some Khalkas have become farmers

The Mongolian Language

Mongolian is not a single language, but rather a group of closely related languages spoken by the various tribes that make up the Mongolian people. The Mongolian languages are usually considered to belong to two groups: Eastern Mongolian, including Khalka, Buriat, and Chakhar; and Western Mongolian, including various Oirat languages and Kalmuk. Within the Mongolian People's Republic (MPR) the influence of nationwide radio and television broadcasting and motion pictures has gradually standardized Khalka as the national language; the Urga dialect (spoken around the capital, Ulan Bator) tends to predominate over local usages.

The Mongolian languages belong to the Uralic-Altaic language family, named for the Ural Mountains of Russia and the Altai Mountains of western Mongolia. Spread by ancient migrations and the conquests of the Mongol Empire itself, the Uralic–Altaic language family is large and diverse; it includes among others Korean and Japanese, Manchu and Mongolian, Turkish, Finnish, and Hungarian. All these languages are characterized by a highly inflected grammar, meaning that grammatical structure is indicated by prefixes, suffixes, vowel shifts, and other changes of words within a sentence.

For example, the Mongolian word for "to grasp," like all verbs in Mongolian, takes on different suffixes according to its specific function:

imperative	*bari*	grasp
present	*barimui*	grasps
future	*barissugai*	will grasp
causative	*barigulkhu*	to cause to grasp
cooperative	*bariltsakhu*	to grasp together

Another key feature of Mongolian is the so-called "harmony of vowels." All vowels in Mongolian are divided into "hard" forms (for example, o, u) and "soft" forms (for example, ö, ü). A word may contain all hard vowels or all soft vowels, but not both forms within the same word.

Traditionally, the Mongolian language was written in a script that had been borrowed from the written language of the Uighurs around the time of Genghis Khan. (The Uighur script itself was adapted from the Sogdian script of Persia, and ultimately from the Aramaic script of ancient Palestine.) The Uighur script was alphabetical, and although it did not perfectly convey the sounds of spoken Mongolian, it remained in use until modern times. The Tibetan language, with its own script, was used for religious writings and certain other formal documents.

Today, traditional Mongolian writing remains in use among the Mongols of China, but within Mongolia and the Mongol regions of the Soviet Union, Mongolian is now written in the Russian Cyrillic alphabet.

English	*Mongolian*	*Cyrillic*
Qing Dynasty (ruled China 1644–1911)	ᠴᡅᠨ	ЧИН

on the large grain-producing state farms of the Mongolian People's Republic; many more have become city and town dwellers, exchanging their steppe lifestyle for that of miners, factory workers, office workers, teachers, doctors, and scientists.

In the Chinese Inner Mongolian Autonomous Region, most of the Mongols are Chakhars; the rest are Oirats, a people traditionally divided into the Eastern Oirat and Western Oirat confederations. The Chakhars and Oirats are peoples of the Gobi and the transitional lands between steppe Mongolia and agricultural China. They are shepherds and camel breeders, caravaneers, sometimes farmers on marginal agricultural lands or in desert oases.

In the seventeenth century, a group of Western Oirat people migrated west to the region south of the Volga River, west of the Caspian Sea, where they became known as the Kalmuks. In the eighteenth century, most migrated back eastward again; their descendants now live in China's Xinjiang Province and, in smaller numbers, in Afghanistan. Those who remained behind now occupy the Kalmytskaya Autonomous Soviet Socialist Republic, a small corner of the Soviet Union south of the city of Volgagrad. (After the 1917 Russian Revolution many of the Volga Kalmuks emigrated to eastern Europe and, after World War II, to the United States; one of the largest Mongolian communities outside Asia is now in New Jersey.)

North of Mongolia, the Buriat Mongols live in the Soviet Union's Buriatskaya Autonomous Soviet Socialist Republic, south and east of Lake Baikal. The Buriats are forest Mongols: hunters, fur trappers, cattle raisers, and marginal farmers. Their homeland is in a small part of the taiga, the vast open forest of birch and evergreen trees that covers all of Siberia south of the tundra and north of the steppe.

Despite long-standing distinctions of tribal identification, and despite significantly different lifestyles (ranging from forest hunters to horse-riding shepherds to camel breeders and, today, from industrial laborers to white-collar workers), all of these groups collectively make up the Mongolian people. More than half of them live outside the Mongolian People's Republic, their wide geographical distribution a reminder of the far-flung Mongol Empire of centuries past.

C H A P T E R I I

The Land

Mongolia is the world's largest landlocked nation. Encompassing an area almost as large as Arizona, New Mexico, Texas, and Louisiana combined, the Mongolian People's Republic (M.P.R.) is bounded on the north by the Soviet Union and on the south by China. It has no navigable rivers, and is entirely cut off from the sea. The terrain, almost all of which lies above 3,000 feet (900 meters), consists primarily of grasslands and desert. It also includes two large mountain ranges, with snow-capped peaks and forested foothills, and several large lakes.

The political boundaries of what is now the Mongolian People's Republic were established, in the north, by treaties between czarist Russia and the Chinese Empire in 1689 and 1727, and, in the south, by agreements between Mongolia and the Republic of China in the early twentieth century. The area within those boundaries, sometimes still called by its old name, Outer Mongolia, includes only about half of the traditional homeland of the Mongolian people, which also covered large territories that are now part of the Soviet Union and the People's Republic of China. Those regions today are still inhabited by large numbers of Mongols, who are culturally and ethnically closely related to the citizens of the Mongolian People's Republic.

The establishment of closed political boundaries in modern times had a profound effect on the cultural and economic life of the Mongols, who were accustomed to migrating and trading over vast distances with no regard for arbitrary lines drawn on maps. The Mongols of the M.P.R. have, in response to the policies of their central government, modified substantially their patterns of living. Cooperative stock farms with well-defined rangelands have largely replaced the old system of migratory tribes; and, just as in the American West, fenced ranches have replaced free-range prairie. In the relatively small portion of the country in which agriculture is possible, huge state-run farms have been created to grow grain and fodder. Cities and towns, insignificant in traditional Mongolia, today house slightly more than half of the population. In general, the population is now far more settled than was the case before modern times.

Population

Mongolia is very sparsely inhabited; its huge territory supports a population of only about 2 million people, with an average population density of a little over three people per square mile—about half the population density of Montana. The population is not evenly distributed, however. More than half a million people live in the capital, Ulan Bator, and a total of more than 400,000 in other cities and towns. Population density is lowest in the Gobi, in the southeast, where some areas, comprising

Mongolia's Geography and Climate

Highest Mountain	Mönh Hayrhan Uul: 14,311 feet (4,362 meters)
Land Under 1000 meters (3280 feet)	Less than 15%
Largest Lakes	Hövsgöl Nuur: area 1,293 square miles (3,350 square kilometers); depth 780 feet (238 meters)
	Uvs Nuur: area 1,011 sq. mi. (2,620 sq. km.); depth unknown
Longest Rivers	Kerulen: length 784 mi. (1,265 km.)
	Orkhon: length 697 mi. (1,124 km.)
	Selenge: length 620 mi. (998 km.)
Average Temperature, January	Khangai: −29° Fahrenheit (−34° Centigrade)
	Gobi: −2° F (−19° C)
Average Temperature, July	Khangai: 59° F (15° C)
	Gobi: 73° F (23° C)
Most Annual Rainfall	Selenge Valley: 20 inches (51 centimeters)
Least Annual Rainfall	Southeastern Gobi: under 2 in. (5 cm.)
Sunny Days per Year	220–260 (nationwide)

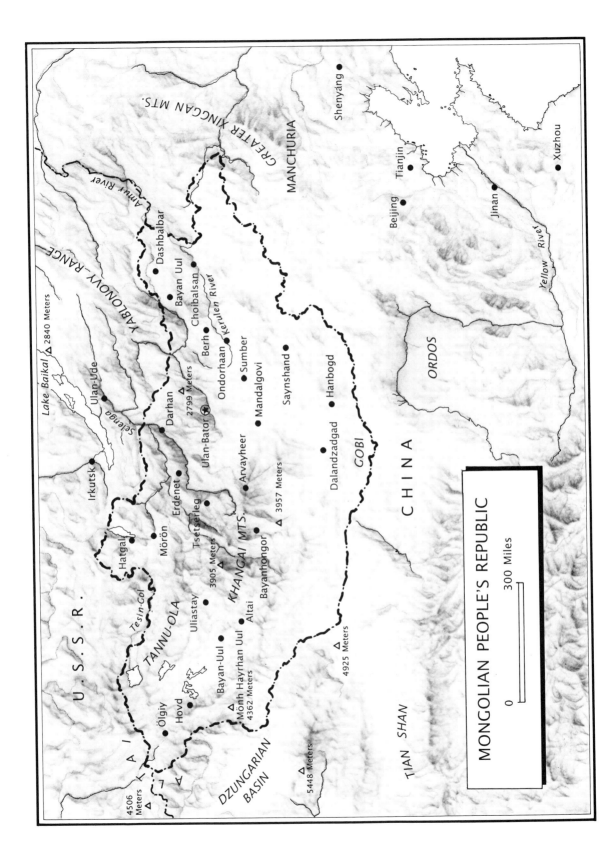

MONGOLIAN PEOPLE'S REPUBLIC

300 Miles

0

salt flats and sand dunes, are essentially uninhabited. The more hospitable steppelands of the northern part of the country are dotted at distant intervals with permanent or semipermanent villages of livestock herders and farmers. The population of domestic animals—sheep, goats, horses, cattle, yaks, and camels—far exceeds that of humans. The human population is growing rapidly, however, impelled by a government policy of encouraging large families; half the people in the country are under twenty-five years of age.

Mongolian herdsmen in about 1920. Migrating with the seasons and taking care of their herds allowed Mongols to raise animals successfully even in the harsh environment of the Gobi. Neg. no. 119124 Courtesy Department of Library Services, American Museum of Natural History

Climate

The climate of Mongolia features sharply defined seasons and wide variations in both daily and seasonal temperatures. Summers are short, with mild days and chilly nights; winters are very long and extremely cold. In all seasons, the wind blows unceasingly across the treeless plains. Precipitation is scarce throughout the country. The western mountains and the northern Selenge Valley receive the most abundant rain and snow; the steppes of the north receive enough moisture to maintain good pastures and to support some agriculture, though crop yields are low. In the Gobi it seldom rains or snows, and only desert vegetation can survive.

Mongolia is divided into two main geographical regions, Khangai and the Gobi. While they share some broad characteristics, each also has its own distinctive features.

Khangai

The Khangai region encompasses the western and northern portions of the country, and takes its name from the Khangai mountain range of west-central Mongolia. The mountains are rugged and high, with peaks ranging from 4,000 feet (1,200 meters) to over 12,000 feet (3,750 meters); the foothills are heavily forested. To the west of the Khangai range, along the western edge of the country and down toward its southwestern corner, is another, and even higher, chain of mountains, the Altai. The Altai range includes Mongolia's highest mountain, Mönh Hayrhan Uul, at 14,311 feet (4,362 meters). When the prevailing northwest winds strike these mountain ranges, the moisture in the rising air condenses and falls as rain or snow.

Both the Khangai and the Altai mountains thus give rise to numerous cold, fast-flowing rivers. From the western Altai Mountains, the Hovd Gol flows into three large lakes—Har Us Nuur, Har Nuur, and Döröö Nuur—that are linked together by short rivers. From the western Khangai, the Dzavhan Gol feeds another large lake, Hyargas Nuur. All four of those lakes, and also the even larger Uvs Nuur farther north, are not drained by any rivers; their water therefore is salty. The rivers that flow from the northern slopes of the Khangai Mountains eventually join the Selenge and Orkhon Rivers, and flow through the steppes to Lake Baikal. The larger rivers and lakes contribute trout, salmon, and sturgeon to the Mongolian diet. Because most moisture falls on the northern slopes of the mountains, few rivers flow southward, and even fewer penetrate the fringes of the Gobi.

North and east of the mountain ranges, the Khangai region becomes a landscape of rolling steppes, uniformly carpeted with short grass and absolutely treeless. This is the region of Mongolia's best pasturelands, and the plains support enormous herds of horses and cattle, flocks of sheep and goats, and, at higher altitudes, herds of yaks. Traditional patterns of migration in this region, from summer to winter pastures and back again, have yielded to a modern system of penning animals during the winter and feeding them on cut fodder. Irrigation (from deep wells) has improved the quality of pastureland in large areas of the Khangai, further reducing the need for seasonal migrations. Herding families now live semisedentary lives, in yurts installed on wooden platforms and with iron stoves in place of dirt fireplaces. The ancient skills of animal husbandry remain, however, as riders range for miles across the rolling hills to control and protect their animals. Trained to the saddle from infancy, fearless and proud of their horsemanship, carrying their distinctive pole-lassoes like the lances of medieval knights, the Mongol riders are perfectly at home in their harsh environment. Their work is rewarded by a rich harvest of meat and hides, wool and milk.

The short grass of the steppe holds moisture well, and is the key to the region's livestock economy. In the springtime, the steppe turns a soft, pale green as the earth thaws and the grass, mixed with the blossoms of a profusion of dwarf wildflowers, begins to grow. During the brief summer, the grass ripens and turns brown; autumn quickly yields to the long and frigid winter. Winter is a trial for humans and animals alike as cold winds from Siberia howl across the plains, bringing subzero temperatures and occasional light snow.

The central Khangai region also provides most of Mongolia's arable land—land that can be plowed and planted. In broad valleys that afford some shelter from the wind, the use of tractors and mechanical harvesters has allowed the establishment of huge state-run farms. Shallow plowing is employed to reduce soil erosion, and deep wells provide water for irrigation. The principal crops are grain and fodder; grain

Aerial view of a state farm near Ulan Bator. Note the large size of the fields, made possible by the use of mechanized equipment.

crops are limited to those, such as wheat, rye, and oats, that can tolerate the region's short growing season and dry, cold climate. These state farms are inefficient, but they do succeed in growing grain where none was grown before.

Although precipitation is never abundant in the Khangai region, north-central Mongolia is crossed by the numerous rivers that arise in the eastern Khangai and other, smaller mountain ranges. These rivers are tributaries of the Orkhon and Selenge Rivers, which eventually merge and flow northward to Lake Baikal. The rivers of the more easterly steppelands flow into the Onon and the Kerulen, which form part of the headwaters of the mighty Amur River.

The eastern steppes are somewhat lower in average elevation, and somewhat drier, than those of the central Khangai region, but are otherwise generally similar. At its easternmost point, the border be-

Yaks thrive only at high altitudes, such as the high steppelands of the western Khangai. Versatile beasts, they are useful pack animals and also yield milk, meat, wool, and leather. Photo: Zuulchin National Travel Agency, M.P.R.

tween Mongolia and China extends into a portion of the Xinggan Mountains. A long chain of mountains running along a north-south line at about 122° east longitude, the Xinggan range formed the traditional boundary between Mongolia and Manchuria (now the three northeastern provinces of China).

While livestock raising, and secondarily agriculture, form the basic economy of the Khangai region, there is some industry as well. The principal industries involve the processing of animal products, such as tanned and finished leather and sheepskin, meat and meat by-products, cheese and other dairy products, woolen carpets, woven and knitted woolen textiles, and garments and shoes. Besides livestock-related industries, there are a number of coal fields, particularly in the area just south of Ulan Bator, and coal is a major export to the Soviet Union. Copper and molybdenum mines in the vicinity of Erdenet have turned that small city into an important ore-processing center. Darhan, on the railway line linking Ulan Bator with Irkutsk in the U.S.S.R., is a center for the production of bricks and other building materials.

Ulan Bator

The capital of Mongolia lies on the Tula River, in the heart of the north-central Khangai steppe. Known in prerevolutionary times as Urga, the old city consisted of a few dusty streets of shops and warehouses, the Chinese-style palace of the local prince, and clusters of permanently installed yurts surrounding the Gandan Monastery and other Buddhist temples. Renamed Ulan Bator ("Red Hero") in 1924, the city was rapidly transformed into the national center of political, economic, and cultural and intellectual life as a showpiece of Soviet-style development. A large central square, surrounded by government buildings, forms the new focus of the city. The old palace is now a

Herdsmen at a collective horse-breeding farm, in the rich steppe pastureland of the central Khangai region.

museum, while the Gandan Monastery continues to dominate the cityscape from its position atop a high hill, maintaining a remnant of religious life in Mongolia's modern secular society.

Ulan Bator is a large and thriving city, but not a particularly attractive one. Apartment buildings made of precast concrete slabs stretch for miles in every direction, housing the rapidly growing population. The clear air of the steppes is fouled by the smoke from four large coal-fired generating stations as well as numerous factories and the exhaust of motor vehicles. Suburbs of yurt villages ring the city, sheltering from the wind behind high wooden walls. For better or for worse, Ulan Bator represents Mongolia's entry into the modern world, as the heirs of nomads and monks now make their living in the sprawling precincts of Mongolia's only large city.

The Gobi

South and east of the Khangai range, the grassy steppe becomes more arid, soon giving way to the vast desert known as the Gobi. The terrain of the Gobi is surprisingly varied, including sand dunes, gravel plains, scrublands, dry prairie, brackish lakes, salt marshes, salt flats, willow breaks, canyonlands, and mountains—most notably the Gurvan Saikhan range near the Chinese border.

The Gobi is sparsely inhabited, but it does contain towns and centers of industry. Coal and fluorspar are mined in several areas. Towns along the main rail line between Ulan Bator and Beijing are centers of trade as well as of railroad work. Other towns serve the needs of widely scattered herding cooperatives. The Gobi also has a large population of soldiers, housed in Soviet and Mongolian military bases along the heavily guarded border with China.

The climate of the Gobi is both more arid and more extreme than that of the steppelands to the north. Winters are bitterly cold. Summer days can be intensely hot, but the temperature drops sharply after nightfall. In the Valley of Yol in the eastern Gurvan Saikhan range, a spring-fed stream runs through a deep canyon; untouched by the sun's rays, the surface of the stream remains frozen year-round.

The economy of the Gobi, like that of the Khangai region, is based primarily on livestock raising. Most of the Gobi is too arid for horses and cattle, however; the main domestic animals of the desert are sheep, goats, and—especially—camels. More than 600,000 domestic camels roam the Gobi, tended by seminomadic herders; the camels are of the Central Asian or Bactrian (two-humped) type, smaller, hardier, and with much thicker wool than the one-humped dromedaries of Arabia and

A herd of Bactrian camels grazing in the scrub desert of the western Gobi.

Mongolian Wildlife

Besides supporting large herds and flocks of domestic animals, the steppes and deserts of Mongolia are rich in wildlife. Notable birds include several types of cranes, a wide range of eagles, hawks, buzzards, and kites, and such wildfowl as great bustards, pheasants, and ptarmigan. Antelope and gazelles graze on the steppes, while argali goats and ibexes are found in the Gobi. The Gobi is also home to wild horses, wild asses, and wild camels. These are not descendants of escaped domestic animals, but rather are true wild species that have never been tamed. An estimated thirty thousand wolves roam the steppes, and Gobi bears are found in the desert. Tigers and snow leopards, though now extremely rare, survive in small numbers in remote areas.

Traditionally, hunting has been an important part of Mongolian life. In prerevolutionary times, falconry, possibly borrowed from Persia, was used in hunting wildfowl and small animals. Mongol hunters used special archery techniques to shoot birds, whether at roost or on the wing. Dogs, and even trained cheetahs, were used to chase down larger game. Sometimes large-scale hunts were organized in which beaters drove whole herds of antelope to the deadly bows of waiting hunters.

Today hunting in Mongolia is strictly regulated; a network of national parks and game reserves has been established. Hunters, armed with rifles rather than bows, are required to have licenses issued by the Ministry of Nature Protection and the Environment. Fur trapping remains a major source of income, and the pelts of marmots, sables, and other animals are exported in large numbers.

The great bustard is one of the largest and most highly prized game birds of the steppe. In premodern times these birds were hunted both with bows and arrows and with falcons. The great bustard is strikingly beautiful, with bold patterns of brown, black, and white, and has a wingspan of almost four feet.

North Africa. The goats of the Gobi, fortified against the cold by their thick underwool, are the world's major source of cashmere yarn. (China's Inner Mongolian Autonomous Region, which encompasses the southern portion of the Gobi, produces more cashmere than does the Mongolian People's Republic.)

Other products of the Gobi include aromatic woods from desert scrub plants, semiprecious stones such as jasper, turquoise, agate, and rock crystal, and, most famously, dinosaur bones and eggs. The heavily eroded sedimentary rock of the Gobi makes it one of the world's richest hunting grounds for fossils.

Transportation and Communications

In premodern times, all freight in Mongolia was carried by camel caravans, pack horses, and oxcarts. The creation of a modern transportation system has therefore been an important priority of the Mongolian government.

The key transportation artery in today's Mongolia is the railroad that runs through the country from north to south, linking Ulan Bator with Irkutsk, in the U.S.S.R. (since 1950), and with Beijing, in China (since 1955). That rail line carries nearly all of Mongolia's vital trade with the Soviet Union and Eastern Europe; it also serves international passenger traffic. Some freight is also carried by a smaller rail line, built in 1939, that links the Soviet Trans-Siberian Railway with Choibalsan and other mining and industrial cities of eastern Mongolia. A network of roads, mostly unpaved, also now connects Mongolia's main cities and

Dr. Roy Chapman Andrews, leader of 1923–1925 American Museum of Natural History Central Asian Expedition, with a nest of fossil dinosaur eggs in the Gobi Desert. Neg. no. 410743 (Photo by Shackelford), Courtesy Department of Library Services, American Museum of Natural History

Genghis Khan's Pony Express

Expert horsemanship gives the Mongols an important means of coping with the vast expanses of their steppe homeland. Mongol children learn to ride in infancy; even before they can walk, they are taught to balance on the back of a sheep, and in early childhood they graduate to riding ponies. Both boys and girls learn to ride, although the work of tending herds from horseback is performed mainly by men.

In the past, Mongol men were warriors and hunters as well as herdsmen, and in all those roles they depended on their skills as riders. Trained to ignore fatigue, a Mongol rider could stay on his horse for hours or even days at a time, adjusting his pace to the strength of the horse and napping in the saddle when necessary. Horse and rider formed a single unit. The rider was independent even of the need to find food; mounted on a healthy mare, he could, if necessary, sustain himself with a nutritious mixture of mare's milk and fresh blood tapped from a vein in the horse's neck.

In the thirteenth century, Genghis Khan maintained control of his continent-spanning empire through the use of a mounted postal system that employed the best horses and most skilled riders in his realm. Relay stations were established on main routes at a distance of about every twenty-five miles to provide fresh horses. "Arrow riders," their bodies wrapped in cloth bandages as protection against the shock of hard riding, raced from station to station. The bells on the horse's harness would alert the station keeper to have a fresh horse ready, so that the rider could continue on without pause. Traveling around the clock, relays of riders would cover up to three hundred miles a day. An urgent message could be carried from Damascus to Karakorum, a distance of at least 3,500 miles, in under two weeks. An ordinary caravan would take at least six months to make the same journey.

towns. Internal freight and passenger traffic generally moves by truck and bus. Ulan Bator airport serves international and domestic air routes, with scheduled service even to small towns with dirt airstrips, though in practice flights are irregular. In the countryside, horses and camels are still the indispensable means of personal transportation, but today they are beginning to be supplemented by the use of motorcycles.

Mongolia's first radio transmitter was established in Ulan Bator in 1934 with Soviet assistance. Radio and television stations in Ulan Bator and other main cities, using Soviet communications satellites, now provide broadcasts to all but the most remote regions of the country.

Steppe Culture and the Rise of the Mongols

The Mongols as a distinct people were relatively late arrivals in Asian history; the word "Mongol" does not appear in historical records before the tenth century A.D. The Mongols seem to have originated in the area between Lake Baikal and the Xinggan Mountains, and gradually spread southward and westward into the Khangai and the Gobi, displacing or mixing with other steppe peoples in the course of their expansion. The specific ethnic identity of the Mongols is less important, however, than their cultural identity. ("Cultural identity" means a sense of belonging to a group on the basis of a shared environment, lifestyle, and set of beliefs. One can be culturally "American" and ethnically Irish, African, or anything else.) As the latest of many waves of people to make their homes on the steppe, the Mongols may originally have been noticeably different from their predecessors, but in adopting the characteristic lifestyle of the steppe, they became culturally nearly indistinguishable from those who had come before.

The Origins of Steppe Culture

Life on the steppe depends fundamentally on the raising of herds of animals. The first moves toward the creation of a pastoral (herding) society in the steppe took place sometime before around 3000 B.C., and paralleled (with a slight time lag) the rise of Neolithic agricultural civilization in China to the south. The Neolithic Period, the New Stone Age, marks a great turning point in human history. In the last phase of pre-Neolithic culture, there was no great difference between the culture of North China and that of the steppes. Small bands of people moved across the land, hunting game and gathering wild plants for food. Gradually, in the middle reaches of the Yellow River, people began to encourage stands of wild grain, and then to practice primitive agriculture. As agriculture developed, villages, then towns, then cities and empires grew, built upon the wealth that they drew from the soil.

North of the North China Plain lies a broad belt of transitional land, in which, as one travels north and toward the interior of the continent, it is more and more difficult to grow crops. The transition is a gradual one, moving from cultivable land to less cultivable land and finally to land in which agriculture is nearly or altogether impossible. In the drier lands of the north, hunting and gathering led, therefore, to a society based on the control of animals—initially, perhaps, the driving of herds of semidomesticated game animals, later the breeding and husbandry of sheep, cattle, and other domestic animals. As the digging stick and the hoe led gradually to full-scale grain cultivation in the south, animal tending led in the north to fully developed pastoral nomadism—a sys-

Pastoral Nomadism

Pastoral nomadism is a distinctive way of life found among many people whose livelihood depends primarily on the raising of domestic animals. Any people who raise animals confront the basic, inescapable fact that the animals must constantly be fed. There are two ways of dealing with this: Bring the food to the animals, or bring the animals to the food. In modern industrialized societies, the former solution is the usual one; animals are kept in barns or fenced yards, and fed with grain and fodder produced elsewhere. But in traditional societies, people usually found it easier to follow their animals from place to place in search of food.

"Pastoralism" refers to the feeding of animals in open pastures. A pasture can produce only a limited amount of grass; when the animals have eaten it, they must move on. Often the movement might be only as far as to another section of the same pasture. But pastures also are seasonal; a field might be green in one season, but snow covered or dried out in another. The changing seasonal availability of food leads to "nomadism," an annual pattern of migration from pasture to pasture. Nomadism takes different forms. In some societies (such as in the Swiss Alps), migrations move from summer pastures in high mountain meadows to winter pastures in lower, sheltered valleys. In other societies (such as the cattle-raising societies of East Africa), the migration covers considerable distances between relatively low-lying winter pastures and somewhat higher summer pastures. In Mongolia, both patterns of migration are found. Migrations might cover only a few miles, or up to hundreds of miles; the important fact is that they are regular and determined by the seasonal availability of pasturage.

Pastoral nomads frequently maintain close relations with nearby settled societies. The nomads depend upon farmers and townspeople for such things as cloth, metal, grain, sugar, salt, and beverages like tea or coffee. To obtain such necessities, the nomads usually trade animal products, such as meat, cheese, and hides, at market centers where the two cultures meet. Sometimes the nomads get what they need by raiding instead, and nomads are often feared by members of more settled societies.

All around the world, pastoral nomadic societies tend to have certain similarities. They are usually tribal in their social organization. Compared with settled societies, there is relatively greater equality between men and women, and between leaders and followers. Certain personal qualities, such as courage, loyalty, and honor, are held in high regard. Wealth is measured in livestock, jewelry, and other portable goods. In the arts, oral literature (such as poetry) and music have greater importance than painting and sculpture.

Like other forms of human culture, pastoral nomadism evolved over a long period of time, and represents a sophisticated and complex response to particular environmental needs.

A cashmere goat. This hardy animal is important to Mongolia's economy because of its undercoat of exceptionally soft wool, highly prized for making cashmere yarn and cloth.

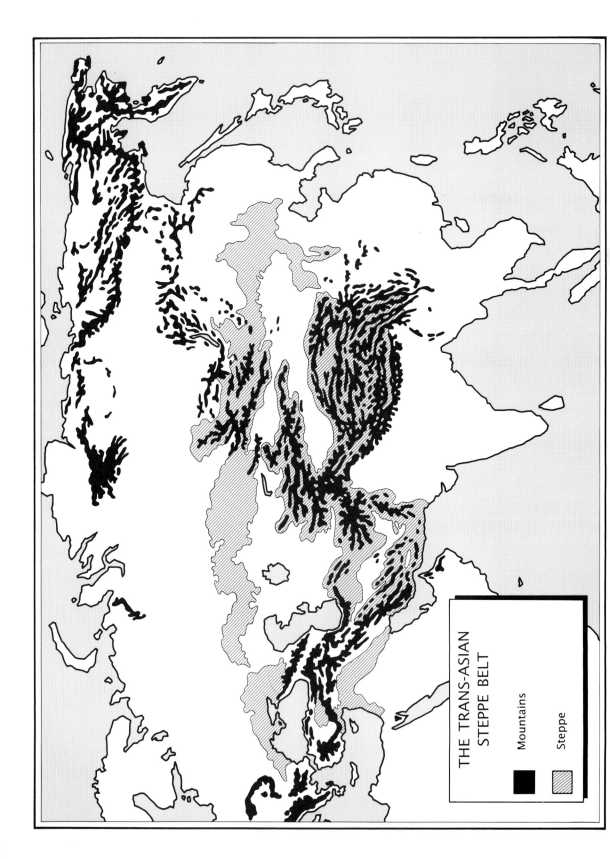

THE TRANS-ASIAN
STEPPE BELT

Mountains

Steppe

tem that is neither older than nor more primitive than agrarian civilization, but simply very different from it.

For many centuries, however, the distinction between the cultivated south and the pastoral north was relative rather than absolute. At least some of the peoples on either side of the transition zone were probably related to each other and spoke similar languages. Early Neolithic Chinese farmers hunted and tended flocks; early steppe herdsmen probably cultivated crops in regions where that was possible. From about 1500 B.C. onward, both societies used horses, but only to pull wheeled vehicles; riding astride still lay far in the future. But with the develop-

Square bronze buckle, with decor showing a stag attacked by predatory animals. Probably from the eastern Baikal region, about 500 B.C. Objects with this kind of "animal style" decor were produced throughout the trans-Asian steppe from about 1000 B.C. to A.D. 1000.
Museum of Fine Arts, Boston

ment of large-scale irrigation and intensive agriculture in China, and of the techniques of horse riding in the north (by around 500 B.C.), the two cultures diverged. Efficiency demanded that each side concentrate on what it did best. On prime cropland, grain was more productive than flocks; on the steppe, herds and flocks had to move in order to eat, and marginal farms became useless anchors. Power in the north came not from the ownership or taxation of land, but from the ability to control migration routes and access to pastures.

The development of pastoral nomadic societies took place not only in Mongolia, but all across the broad belt of steppelands and desert that spans Asia from the Xinggan Mountains in the east to the Carpathian Mountains in the west. The topography and climate of inner Asia led to the growth of similar cultures throughout its expanse. The Scythians, a tribe of wagon-dwelling, mare-milking nomads living north of the Black Sea, were known and feared by the Greeks. They were closely related, culturally if not ethnically, to such tribes in Mongolia and Xinjiang as the Wusun and the Yuezhi, with whom the Chinese were in contact at the same time. The distribution throughout Central Asia of jewelry and horse trappings decorated in the so-called "Scythian" or "animal style" of art testifies to the broad unity of steppe culture and to its success as an alternative to the agrarian civilizations of China, Persia, and the Middle East.

Horse Riders of the Steppes

Mobility was the key link in the development of steppe society. Anything that could not readily be carried on a migration was a burden. Sheep were the source of milk, meat, wool, and skins, but sheep could not remain long on a single steppe pasture without the danger of overgrazing. Horse riding—which supplemented the use of horses as

Decorated felt and leather saddle blanket from a tomb at Pazyrik, South Siberia, about 400 B.C. By the middle of the first millennium B.C., mounted warriors had transformed the scattered steppe tribes into formidable fighting forces. The Hermitage Museum, Leningrad

Glazed terra-cotta statuette of a heavily laden Bactrian camel and a Turkish caravaneer, Tang Dynasty China, eighth century A.D. Small ceramic sculptures like this one were used as funeral offerings in China, and were buried in tombs. The Tang Dynasty extended its control far out into Central Asia and vigorously promoted trans-Asian trade along the Silk Route; caravans of pack camels, tended by Central Asian merchants, would have been a common sight in the capital city of Chang'an. Neg. no. 98631, Courtesy Photography Department, Field Museum of Natural History, Chicago

draft and dairy animals—developed over a long period of time; it required new techniques for taming horses to the saddle, the creation of appropriate harness and equipment, and the invention and transmission of difficult skills. When steppe nomads learned to be at home in the saddle, they took the final step in establishing a distinctive lifestyle of their own. Expert horsemen could control larger flocks of sheep, and therefore could become wealthy in the only terms that had meaning on the steppe. They could defend their migration routes and pastures, hunt from horseback when the opportunity presented itself, and carry out raids against any settled people within striking distance.

The Roman historian Sidonius, in the fifth century A.D., described the invading Huns in terms that could be applied to any of the peoples of the steppe:

Scarce had the infant learnt to stand without his mother's aid when a horse takes him on his back. You would think that the limbs of man and horse were born together, so firmly does the rider always stick to the horse; any other folk is carried on horseback, this folk lives there.

Commerce, industry, and agriculture remained on a small scale or were entirely lacking in the territories controlled by the nomads, because any accumulation of wealth gained through such activities would quickly be stolen by mounted raiders who were not tied down by permanent dwellings and heavy equipment. Artisans—blacksmiths, wheelwrights, armorers, and the like—traveled with their tribes and practiced their crafts en route. Merchants were often outsiders, bringing agricultural products and manufactured goods—particularly metal and silk—to the steppe, where they were exchanged at seasonal fairs for livestock and animal products. Sometimes, too, groups of nomads led caravans to towns in the border regions to exchange their goods for the products of settled society.

The development of horsemanship on the steppe was complemented by the development of the short, powerful compound bow that lent heavy firepower to the defenders of flocks and raiders of settlements. The stirrup was a surprisingly late development—certainly no earlier than A.D. 200—that improved horsemanship and made mounted archery more deadly; it refined the techniques of steppe society but was not essential to their creation. By the third century B.C., the mounted warriors of the steppe had already become a force to be feared on China's northern frontier. The peoples whom the Chinese had long called by a variety of names, all of which meant "barbarian," were now no longer simply "backward": They were distinctly different, and dangerous.

The Great Wall of China

The broad transitional zone on China's northern frontier was potentially suitable both for grazing land and for agriculture. The temptation for Chinese governments was to push the limits of grain cultivation—and land taxation—as far north as was feasible; the nomads, in contrast, tried to pasture their flocks as far south as they could. The Great Wall of China, completed in 213 B.C. largely by linking together shorter segments of earlier walls, was an attempt to create a definite border in the transitional zone; it said, in effect, that peace would be maintained by keeping farmers on the inside of the wall, and nomads on the outside. But over the long run, the wall proved to be only a poor barrier against the expansionist tendencies of two very different, and competing, societies. Whenever Chinese governments felt strong enough to do so, they tried to drive the herdsmen far to the north of the wall, establishing farms and military garrisons at the southern edge of the Gobi. Time and again throughout history, horsemen swept south across the wall to plunder and sometimes to conquer.

The Dynamics of Steppe Society

Pastoral nomadism tends to produce what anthropologists call segmentary societies—societies that are organized in a hierarchy of families, clans, tribes, and confederations. Segmentation means that societies organize themselves into the smallest units that will work efficiently and effectively for any given task. For example, during an annual spring or fall migration, the basic unit might be the tribe, as everyone involved requires the leadership skills, defensive power, and organization of cooperative labor needed to move thousands of animals over a distance of tens or hundreds of miles. Upon arriving at the seasonal pasture, however, the tribe will quickly fragment into clans, and further into families, because those smaller units can tend their flocks with relative ease and security in a small part of the tribe's grazing lands. The largest unit of organization, the tribal confederation, appears only occasionally, in response to an external threat or an opportunity for plunder and conquest; the strength and duration of the confederation directly mirrors the strength and duration of the crisis or opportunity. A proverb of the Bakhtiyari tribe of Iran aptly summarizes the nature of segmentary nomadic societies everywhere: "Me, my brother, and my cousin against the world; me and my brother against my cousin; me against my brother."

Under such circumstances, leadership exists only with the consent of those who follow, and is accepted only insofar as members of the group feel a need for it. Leadership rests primarily on the respect gained through wisdom, courage, skill, and the demonstrated ability to deliver successful results; it derives only secondarily from hereditary family prestige. Leaders might order, but followers need not obey; the option of leaving the group to follow another leader is always available. Social classes existed—a warrior elite, ordinary herders, artisans, and slaves who worked as craftsmen, laborers, and servants—but they were relatively fluid, so that good or bad luck, personal initiative or its absence, could give rise to a rapid change in status.

Tribal affiliation in Mongolia, as in other steppe societies, was often indicated visually by distinctive differences in hats, clothing, horse blankets, and other personal articles, and also by the heavy jewelry and elaborate headdresses worn by women on formal occasions. This provided a ready means of distinguishing between fellow tribe members and outsiders, friends and foes. In common with many nomadic peoples all over the world, the wealth of Mongolian families was often stored in the form of the women's jewelry, which is easily portable and readily displayed, and which could quickly be sold or exchanged for other goods if the need arose.

In pastoral nomadic societies, women characteristically play an important role—one that is different from that of men, but also a source of honor and respect. Because men might often be away from the grazing lands for long periods of time—hunting, defending flocks and migration routes, or raiding—women took care of hearth and home, tended the flocks, and governed in the absence of male leaders. The wives and daughters of conquered enemies might well be treated as simple booty, to be kept or given away, enslaved or sold, but once she was incorporated into a new family and tribe, the woman's place would again be secure. (The same applied to young boys who were captured in warfare.) Life on the steppe is difficult and dangerous; society requires the contribution of every member and thus develops an appreciation for the roles of men and women, children, adults, and the elderly. Women often learned to become expert riders and fighters. Several times during the history of Mongolia, women became rulers of tribal confederations.

The Dynamics of the Chinese Frontier

China and the tribes of the steppe were normally armed and vigilant, each against the other. The Chinese sought to balance, or outweigh, the nomads' mobility and striking power with larger armies, more firepower (the Chinese crossbow could easily fell a horse), and superior military organization. The Chinese also adopted the cavalry techniques of the nomads themselves, though, understandably, they seldom became as expert as the nomads. When power on both sides of the Great Wall was roughly in balance, peace might reign for long periods at a time. When Chinese governments sensed that the nomads had become divided and vulnerable, or when they felt that the tribes were becoming too threatening, Chinese armies would attack across the wall and attempt to drive the nomads back. Conversely, a tribal confederation could arise on fairly short notice—a matter of months or a few years—to exploit any sign of weakness on the Chinese side.

Chinese military campaigns north of the wall were often successful, sometimes spectacularly so; yet they were incapable of bringing lasting relief from the danger posed by steppe society. Complete victory would send whole tribes on permanent migrations westward, displacing other peoples in their path; the void would quickly be filled by the expansion of new tribes on the fringes of the steppe. Moreover, Chinese victories were often won by diplomacy as well as arms, using the old strategy of "using barbarians to control barbarians"; often the Chinese rulers would find that, when victory was won, their nomad allies would quickly fill the power vacuum on the steppe and re-emerge as enemies in their turn. With good reason, the security of the northern frontier was the single most important external problem for China's rulers for many centuries—from the beginning of dynastic government in China in the second millennium B.C. to the first serious

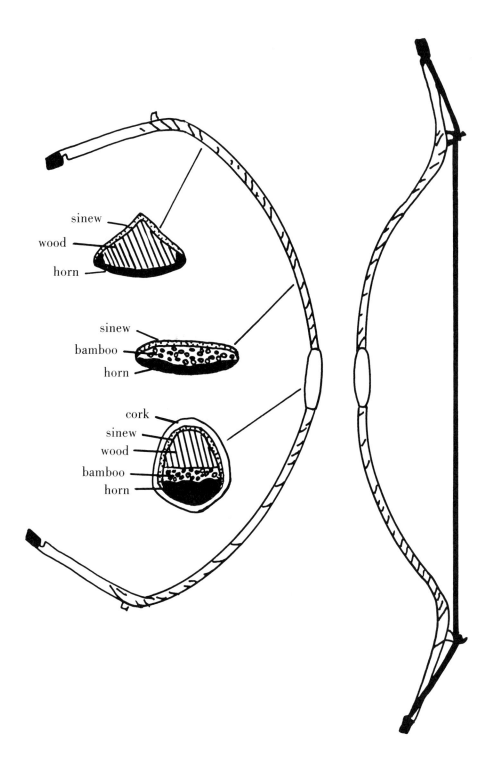

sinew
wood
horn

sinew
bamboo
horn

cork
sinew
wood
bamboo
horn

impact of Europe on China in the eighteenth century A.D.

Chinese governments, in periods of military decline, often tried to bribe the northern nomads into maintaining the peace. Treasure caravans of material goods and even royal brides for the nomad elite were sent northward beyond the wall by many of China's emperors. Embassies of nomads often arrived in the Chinese capital, bearing goods that the Chinese liked to think of as "tribute," but which were, in fact, barely disguised demands for far more valuable Chinese imperial "gifts" in return. This policy of appeasement was self-defeating in the long run; eventually the Chinese would have to defend the frontier by force of arms once again.

The frontier posed a problem for the nomads as well, however. When China appeared vulnerable, the temptation to attack might be irresistible. But nomads were seldom able to carry out campaigns of conquest and long-term territorial control. Border raiding, sometimes on a large scale, might produce short-term gains, but when the opportunity for further plunder diminished, a confederation would dissolve as warriors simply went home again. Besides, if too much power was concentrated on the Chinese border, the steppe itself was open to raids from other tribes. Finally, raiding involved the risk of provoking retaliation when

The Mongolian compound bow. *The compound bow (so called because it was made of a number of different materials) was undoubtedly the product of a long evolutionary development in prehistoric times; it had become the primary hunting and military weapon of the steppe nomads by around 500 B.C. The compound bow was made of wood, bamboo, horn, and sinew; the various materials were fastened together with glue made from boiled fish skin. The shape of the bow in cross section varied continuously from tip to grip. This sophisticated design and construction gave the bow both great strength and great flexibility. Unstrung, the bow recurved sharply in the opposite direction, so that when it was strung, it was under considerable tension even before it was drawn. Fully drawn, the bow would propel an arrow for hundreds of yards with deadly force.* After Denwood, *Arts of the Eurasian Steppelands* (London, The Percival David Foundation, 1978)

China's rulers awoke from their lethargy.

Another temptation of the frontier was to establish bicultural states in the transition zone, with mounted—but no longer nomadic—tribesmen setting themselves up as a ruling elite over the Chinese farming population. But such attempts never worked for very long; the resentful and rebellious Chinese population was difficult to control, while the rulers tended to become cut off from the steppe heartland which then would be taken over by other tribes.

A final option open to warriors on the border, on the rare occasions when a combination of Chinese internal disorder and tribal charismatic leadership made it possible, was to carry out a full-scale conquest of China, abandon the steppe entirely, and settle down to rule China in the manner of a Chinese dynasty, supervising a vast civil bureaucracy and collecting land taxes. That route was followed several times throughout the two thousand years of the Chinese Empire, most successfully by the Manchu rulers of China's last dynasty, the Qing (1644–1911). But its success depended on the conquerers' willingness to give up a substantial part of their own identity as nomadic people of the steppe.

A stable balance of power along China's northern frontier was beneficial to Chinese and nomads alike. Yet over the long run, instability was more common than stability. Clans and tribes with fierce rivalries, long memories, and proud warriors could not keep the peace for long. The persistent ebb and flow of power in the borderlands set the stage for the rise of the Mongols. As other tribes had done in the past, they took control of the steppe behind the back of a larger tribe preoccupied on the Chinese frontier.

The Background of the Mongol Empire

Historical Succession of the Steppe Tribes

The first great tribal confederation of the Mongolian steppe was that of the Hunnu (whom the Chinese called the Xiongnu), at the end of the third century B.C. A tribal leader named Tumen, and his son Maodun, put together a confederation of tribes that began to make increasingly serious raids into the transition zone and northern China itself. They also defeated an unrelated steppe tribe called the Yuezhi, who migrated westward all the way to Bactria, between the Syr Darya and Amu Darya rivers south of the Aral Sea, where they came into direct contact with Greek colonies left over from the conquests of Alexander the Great nearly two centuries before. In a process typical of tribal confederations, after the death of Maodun a crisis of leadership arose; between 180 and 160 B.C. the Hunnu empire split into eastern and western segments, leaving both open to the combined force of Chinese diplomacy and military power.

In 138 B.C. the Chinese sent an ambassador, Zhang Qian, westward to Bactria to try to form an alliance with the Yuezhi against the Hunnu. The Yuezhi, comfortable in their new lands, were unenthusiastic about renewing the battle against their old enemies, but the Chinese neverthe-less embarked on a series of campaigns against the Hunnu, defeating them decisively in 105 B.C. A large number of Hunnu then set out upon a long westward migration over the course of many generations; they showed up on the eastern bank of the Danube in the late fourth century A.D. as the Huns. Although the name of Attila the Hun became, for the Romans, a synonym for barbarian ferocity, the Hunnu were by then far removed from their "barbarian" roots on the Mongolian steppe.

The Hunnu who remained in Mongolia after their great defeat in 105 B.C. were largely displaced by another steppe tribe, the Xianbi. Both groups exploited the weakness of China following the collapse of the Han Empire in A.D. 220. Both Hunnu and Xianbi tribal leaders estab-lished a series of short-lived Chinese-style dynasties in the borderlands and in northern China itself over the next two centuries. In doing so, they gradually lost control of their own original homelands, paving the way for the rise to power in the steppes of yet another group of nomads, the Turks.

Meanwhile, the dominant "barbarian" influence in China at the time came not from Mongolia, but from the forests and river valleys of Manchuria. The Toba people, the first of several Manchurian tribes that would control some or all of China, established the Northern Wei Dynasty in 386 and ruled the North China Plain until 534. The example of a nomadic tribe successfully adopting the Chinese imperial style of rule, including the establishment of a capital city, the use of a civil bureaucracy, and the sponsorship of an organized religion (Buddhism),

THE SHIFTING BALANCE OF POWER IN MONGOLIA

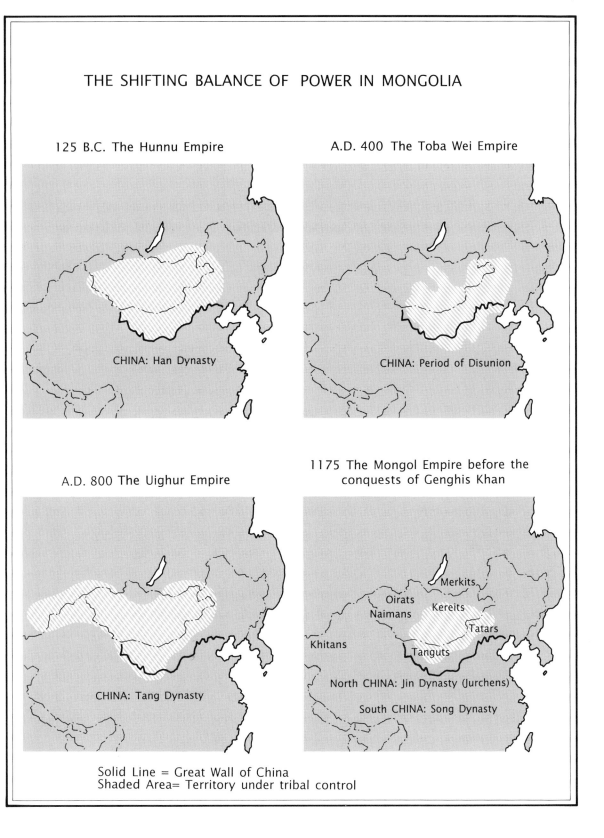

125 B.C. The Hunnu Empire

CHINA: Han Dynasty

A.D. 400 The Toba Wei Empire

CHINA: Period of Disunion

A.D. 800 The Uighur Empire

CHINA: Tang Dynasty

1175 The Mongol Empire before the conquests of Genghis Khan

Merkits
Oirats
Naimans
Kereits
Tatars
Khitans
Tanguts
North CHINA: Jin Dynasty (Jurchens)
South CHINA: Song Dynasty

Solid Line = Great Wall of China
Shaded Area= Territory under tribal control

was noted with interest by the Turkish chieftains who were rising to power on the steppes.

Empires of the Steppes

The Northern Wei Dynasty of the Toba conquerers fell in 534, during a period of dynastic warfare that would lead to the reunification of all of China under ethnic Chinese rule in 589. The Hunnu and Xianbi had long since declined into insignificance. In their place, a series of Turkish leaders had formed their own confederation and, for the first time in history, established a unified, imperial state (modeled on that of the Chinese) in the steppe itself. From 552 to 744 a series of Turkish *khaghans* ruled from imperial palaces in their capital city, aided by a bureaucracy of civilian administrators and by a national network of Buddhist temples whose monks supported the government with their religious authority. The dominant tribe of this empire was Turkish, but its subjects included many different peoples, both tribal and, in the Chinese borderlands, urban and agricultural, who spoke a variety of languages.

In 744, the steppe empire of the Turks was overthrown by another Turkish-speaking tribe, the Uighurs; as many tribes had done before, the Turks set off on a long westward migration, while the Uighurs took over the reins of imperial power in the steppe. The Uighurs dismissed the Buddhist clergy in favor of Manichæan priests, but otherwise ruled exactly as their predecessors had done.

The Turkish and Uighur empires in what is now Mongolia were hybrid states, existing in the midst of pastoral nomadic societies but ruling in a way that had never before proved appropriate to the steppe environment. The ruling elite originated from the nomadic warrior class, but their urban workers—bureaucrats, artisans, merchants, and so on—were almost all foreigners. Chinese administrators kept the account books in the palace offices; Sogdian astrologers from eastern Persia worked in the royal observatory; Syrian and Armenian caravan drivers brought luxury goods from western Asia.

The steppe empires were parasitic states, in the sense that they cost much more than the economy of the steppe itself could support. Palaces, cities, temples, and the extravagant lifestyles of the ruling classes needed an external source of support. This additional wealth came from China. The Sui (589–618) and Tang (618–907) dynasties were unified, powerful, phenomenally rich, and interested in expanding the empire. Their governments needed war-horses for their cavalry and caravaneers for their Silk Route trade; their elites wanted leopard and sable furs and other steppe luxuries. The Chinese had enough money, power, and

A Chinese princess on her way to the steppe to become the bride of a nomadic tribal ruler; she is a pawn in the diplomatic maneuvers used by the emperors of China to maintain peace on their northern frontier. Although this painting, from the narrative hand scroll "Eighteen Songs of a Nomad Flute," refers to the true historical story of Lady Wen Ji—in the Han Dynasty (206 B.C.–A.D. 221)—it accurately depicts the clothing and other details of Mongolia at the time it was painted, in the fourteenth century. Metropolitan Museum of Art

self-confidence to be able to ignore the cost of bribes paid to their northern neighbors in return for peace on the frontier. Because the steppe empires depended on a flow of wealth northward from China, however, their days were numbered when the Tang Dynasty itself entered a long period of decline during the ninth century. In 840, the Uighurs were defeated by another small Turkic tribe, the Kirgiz, and driven westward into Central Asia. Three centuries of unified control on the steppe had come to an end.

The Origins of the Mongols

For three hundred years after the fall of the Uighurs, the steppe reverted to its more typical pattern of tribal rule. No grand confederation arose to exploit the weakness of North China in the tenth century; that opportunity was seized instead by the Manchurian Khitan people, who established their Liao Dynasty in the North China Plain, and by the Tibetan Tangut people, whose state of Xixia dominated northwestern China. On the steppe itself, a number of tribes began to emerge into prominence: The Kereits in the Orkhon River valley, the Merkits in the north-central steppe south of Lake Baikal, the Oirats west of Lake Baikal, the Tatars of eastern Mongolia, and the Naimans in the Altai Mountain region. It is not clear which, if any, of these tribes the Chinese historians of the tenth century had in mind as they began to refer to a northern people called the Mengku, but over the course of the next two centuries, all of them would become part of the Mongol confederation.

The genealogy of Genghis Khan goes back to just this time when the Mongols were beginning to emerge into the consciousness of the outside world. Genghis Khan, whose boyhood name was Temujin, was probably born in 1162; *The Secret History of the Mongols* lists ten generations of his ancestors, which would put the founding of his line sometime around the end of the tenth century. His great-grandfather, though himself a member of a relatively small tribe, had labored to unite the tribes of northern and western Mongolia into the early nucleus of the Mongol confederation, in part for mutual defense against their stronger and more numerous enemies, the Tatars, to the east. Around the same time, the Tangut Xixia state had become established in China's Gansu Province, and the descendants of the Uighurs held the lands south of the Altai. In the early twelfth century the Khitan Liao Dynasty was defeated by another Manchurian tribe, the Jurchens, who conquered North China, established their own Jin Dynasty, and drove the Chinese Song Dynasty south to the Yangtse River. The surviving Khitans retreated westward, setting up the small kingdom of Kara-Khitai in what is now China's Xinjiang Province and Soviet Kazakhstan. The chessboard of the steppe and the borderlands was set up; the pieces were in place. To play the game, a penniless fourteen-year-old orphan, the boy Temujin, stepped onto the stage of history.

The Conquests
of Genghis Khan

The historical process that led to the unification of all of the Mongol tribes began with a by now familiar episode—an attempt by a Chinese dynasty to play one steppe tribe off against another. In 1148, the Jurchen Jin Dynasty of North China began paying "gifts" (bribes) to a confederation of tribes—Kereits, Merkits, and others, by then loosely known as the Mongols—in north-central Mongolia, in return for peace on China's northern frontier. Shortly thereafter, the Jin Dynasty also concluded an alliance with the Tatars, the most powerful tribe of eastern Mongolia, in the hope that they in turn would control the wilder and more hostile Mongols of the confederation.

The Mongol leader, Qabul Khan, had had considerable success in forging his tribal alliance, but after his death, things rapidly began to fall apart under the combined pressure of the Tatars and the Jin. His successor, Ambaqai, was captured by the Tatars and turned over to the Jin to be executed. The next Mongol leader, Qutula, carried out campaign after campaign against the Tatars, with little success; after every defeat, his leadership became more insecure. In one of those campaigns a nephew of Qutula, Yesugei, captured and executed several Tatar chieftains. Later (in about 1176; the date is uncertain), Yesugei was lured to a Tatar camp, ostensibly to discuss peace; he was poisoned instead. At the time his young son, Temujin, was in the camp of one of Yesugei's allies, meeting the girl whom his father had arranged for him to marry.

Temujin hurried back to Yesugei's camp, only to find his father already dead. Yesugei's allies had given him their personal loyalty, but that did not extend to his son; Temujin, though a great-grandson of the mighty Qabul Khan, was judged too young and inexperienced to assume his father's mantle.* Yesugei's followers broke camp and left to seek the leadership of other chiefs; Temujin was robbed of his flocks and left to face the winter with almost no resources. His followers included only his mother, three younger brothers and a sister, two half-brothers, and a handful of other women, young children, and servants.

Defying the death that seemed his probable fate, Temujin and his formidable mother, Hogelun, kept the small band together, endured cold and starvation, and survived. The next summer Temujin murdered his older half-brother, his only rival for leadership in the small camp, and loudly proclaimed his intention of seeking revenge against his father's enemies. Seeing the boy as a possible future threat, one of Yesugei's old allies kidnaped him and held him prisoner for several weeks. During his captivity, Temujin's remarkable personality exerted itself; he won friends in the camp of his captors, who then helped him to escape. Picking up the trail of his mother, he rejoined her camp deep

---

*The year of Temujin's birth is uncertain. Many scholars believe that he was born in 1167 rather than 1162. If so, he would have been only nine years old when his father died, making his rise to leadership even more remarkable.

in the Khangai Mountains. Over the next few years Temujin, at the head of a small group of followers, rebuilt his herds of horses and flocks of sheep through skillful raids against his enemies, claimed his long-betrothed bride (and the backing of her father), and acquired a growing reputation for bravery and determination. In the tradition of steppe leadership, Temujin retained the loyalty of his followers through his success, and by sheer force of character. His closest personal allies became his *anda*, or blood brothers; other followers became *nökhör*, "comrades," who renounced their own families and became honorary members of Temujin's clan.

Temujin devoted himself to what was to become a lifetime of warfare. Steadily defeating his enemies in battle after battle, and attracting allies

The Death of Yesugei

As he rode back Yesugei came on a camp of the Tatar,
who were feasting below Mount Chegcher on the Yellow Steppe.
Tired and thirsty, he dismounted to join in the feasting.
But the Tatar recognized who he was, and said to themselves:
"Yesugei of the Kiyan clan is among us here."
They remembered the times he'd defeated them in battle.
Secretly they decided to kill him,
mixing poisons into the drinks he was offered.
On his way back he felt something was wrong
and after riding three days to get back to his tent
he knew he was dying.
Yesugei the Brave spoke from his bed, saying,
"I feel that I'm dying.

in the process, by the time he was thirty years old he and his core supporters dominated the strategic Onon Valley region in northeastern Mongolia. The large Merkit and Kereit tribes to the west, having themselves felt his ferocity in battle, warily acknowledged his power. In 1194 the Jin Dynasty of North China grew fearful of their old allies, the Tatars. Turning against the Tatars, the Jin rulers concluded an alliance with Temujin, together with his blood brother, the Kereit leader Jamuqa, to conduct a joint campaign against them. The Tatars were defeated and almost annihilated. The armies of Temujin and Jamuqa went on to defeat the Merkits in 1197 and the Turkish Naiman tribe of southwestern Mongolia in 1199.

In 1200, Jamuqa broke with Temujin and put together a confedera-

Who's here beside me?"
Someone answered him:
"Munglig, the son of Old Man Charakha is here."
Yesugei called the boy over to him and said:
"Munglig, my child, my sons are still very young.
As I rode back from leaving Temujin with his wife's family
I was secretly poisoned by the Tatar.
I can feel that I'm dying now.
Take care of my sons like they were your own little brothers.
Take care of my wife like she was your own elder sister.
Go quickly now, Munglig, and bring Temujin back."
Then Yesugei passed away.

From *The Secret History of the Mongols: The Origin of Chinggis Khan*, An Adaptation by Paul Kahn (San Francisco: North Point Press, 1984), pp. 16–17.

tion of all of his former *anda*'s enemies. In 1201, a meeting *(quriltai)* of tribal chiefs proclaimed Jamuqa Grand Khan of all the steppes. Temujin, at the head of his own tribe, was left with only one ally, a section of the Kereit tribe under his old but unreliable friend, Ong Khan. At the end of 1201, the armies met in a snowstorm; Jamuqa was defeated but managed to escape from the battlefield. Temujin followed up this victory with a campaign against the surviving Tatars, who were wiped out as a tribe in 1202. (This is literally true. Except for a few useful artisans, all male Tatar prisoners standing taller than the axle of Temujin's wagon were slaughtered. Women and small children were enslaved.) Temujin was thus in total control of eastern Mongolia. Ong Khan and the Kereits, caught between Temujin in the east and the Naimans in the west, felt the danger of their position and joined with Jamuqa and his surviving forces to try to halt the expanding power of Temujin.

The armies met in 1203 in another bloody but indecisive battle. Temujin withdrew northward into the Baikal steppe, while Jamuqa deserted Ong Khan and headed west. Hearing of this retreat, Temujin attacked again, defeating Ong Khan's army on the banks of the Kerulen River. Ong Khan escaped and sought refuge with the Naiman tribe; the Naiman leader refused to believe that the battered fugitive was Ong Khan, and had him executed. Realizing that their turn would come next, the Naimans moved east from the Altai Mountains to confront Temujin; their forces were joined by Jamuqa, who had gathered a new band of followers. Warned by his spies of the Naimans' approach, Temujin surprised them at the Orkhon River and won a great victory. Those Naimans who survived the carnage retreated westward out of Mongolia to what is now Russian Turkestan. At the end of 1205, Temujin was the undisputed leader of all of Mongolia.

In the following year, Temujin's success was recognized at another *quriltai* of the Mongol chiefs, which proclaimed him Khan (leader) of

all the Mongols. Temujin selected for himself the title Genghis, probably derived from a Turkish word meaning "ocean"; the implication was
that his power spread over the world like a great body of water. His first
act as ruler was to send emissaries to all the steppe tribes, far beyond
the Mongolian homeland itself, to ensure that he had the backing of all
of the "dwellers in felt tents." Except for the still-hostile Naimans, no
one objected. Having satisfied himself on that score, he was ready to
turn his attention to the borderlands of China.

From Confederation to Empire

Genghis Khan had won, but what now? His armies needed new enemies
to conquer, new cities to plunder. If he could not provide his warriors
with the excitement of battle and the spoils of conquest, they would
simply drift away to their own pasturelands and tend their herds. His
confederation had to find new goals, or it would collapse.

Realizing this, Genghis Khan confronted the problem in two ways.
First, he undertook a reorganization of steppe society itself, transform-
ing a traditional tribal confederation into a political and military empire.
His chief followers were given grants of pasturelands and animals, and
also were turned into the leaders of a military aristocracy. The clan
structure of society was reorganized so that each of these leaders received the title of *orlok*, or "general," and was placed in command of
tightly organized cavalry units called *toumans*, each with ten thousand
riders. Every *touman* was divided into ten brigades of a thousand riders,
each with its own commander; and those were further divided into
companies and squadrons. Military discipline was tight; if anyone attempted to flee from the battlefield, he was to be killed by his own
companions. Genghis Khan organized his own elite bodyguard unit
made up of ten thousand of the best warriors of all the tribes; each one

نوریلتای بوزرک جنکیزخان نومی سیده نه باید نصب فرهوز ولتب جنکیزخان رو یه مقدر

کث وعزیمت اویجک بیروق باذتاه کیده بینه ایمان ولدنتن بروزق خان بند کورا جون مبارکی وفرخی مارس سال کسال یوز مانید سوافت

ماه رجب سنه ناین وسنماه مجری در آندیم درا واید مظل جار جنکیزخان فرهوز مانوفی نه باید سید بنای کردنده محبتای باعطت

نوریلتای بنبل ساخت ودران نوریلتای لتب بزرک جنکیزخان بروی معزرکردند وسارکی بربخت بنشت

of them pledged to protect the Khan with his own life. At the same time, the proclamations and judgments of Genghis Khan began to form the basis of the *yasa*, his code of laws; thus a system of government emerged to replace the purely voluntary system of leadership and alliance that had characterized steppe society in the past.

The second part of Genghis Khan's strategy was to employ this formidable military force immediately, so as to reward his followers' loyalty. He found his first target in the Xixia Kingdom in the western borderlands of China's Gansu Province. The Xixia Kingdom was ruled by a Tangut Tibetan elite, and included a mixed population of Chinese and Turks. Although the rulers had come from a tribal society, they had settled down into a pattern of Chinese-style rule over walled towns, farmlands, and trade routes. In 1207, Genghis Khan led his army south across the Gobi to attack the Xixia. This campaign presented the Mongol riders with an unpleasant surprise. Able to pillage at will in the Xixia countryside, they had no experience at all in attacking walled cities, which were able to resist a mounted attack with ease. After an inconclusive season in the battlefield, Genghis Khan had to be content with collecting tribute from the Xixia king, while he withdrew to the steppe to learn about siege warfare.

Mongol riders who were accustomed to lightning raids now had to practice (with the advice of captured Chinese and Turkish military engineers) the use of siege towers, catapults, scaling ladders, tunneling, and other unfamiliar techniques of doing battle against fortified cities. Each of Genghis Khan's top aristocrats was required to provide a fully trained siege unit. At the same time, the more traditional military skills of the Mongols were not neglected; armies were sent eastward to raid

A medieval Persian manuscript illustration showing Genghis Khan holding court in his yurt. Bibliothèque Nationale, Paris

the Khitans in Manchuria, and westward against the Naimans in Turkestan. Jochi, the eldest son of Genghis Khan, led his army against the "forest nomads" north of the Aral Sea; he would spend the rest of his life campaigning in the western regions of Asia.

In 1208–1209 the Mongol armies again attacked Xixia, employing their new siege techniques with some success, although without achieving the total defeat of the kingdom; Xixia was to be a thorn in the side of the Mongols for another two decades. But by 1211, Genghis Khan was confident enough of his ability to conquer cities to embark on a campaign against China itself. In that year he attacked Beijing, the capital of the Jurchen Jin Dynasty that controlled all of northern China. The Mongols had no difficulty in devastating the countryside around the capital, but the city itself was stubbornly defended. For four years the city held out, while the Mongols pressed their attack. Genghis Khan also made an alliance with the Khitans of Manchuria, which forced the Jin to send armies off to the northeastern frontier, weakening their defense of Beijing. In 1215, the starving garrison of the city rebelled and its governor committed suicide; the Mongol army finally marched through the city gates and plundered the Jin capital. For weeks, cartloads of silk, gold, jewelry, and other treasure moved in an endless caravan to the camp of Genghis Khan, along with enslaved captives whose skills were regarded as useful to the Mongols.

One such captive proved to be the greatest treasure of all: the Khitan prince Yelu Qucai, a young bureaucrat in the service of the Jin Dynasty, who was to become one of the most influential of Genghis Khan's advisors. Yelu Qucai taught Genghis Khan that in dealing with agricultural territories, taxation was a more reliable source of wealth than plunder. In teaching the Mongols the lessons of bureaucratic administration, he greatly enriched their empire and also undoubtedly averted much needless looting and slaughter in the lands they conquered.

Thereafter, Genghis Khan left the campaign in northern China in the hands of his general, Muqali. A Jin counterattack in 1218 was repulsed, and in 1221 Muqali concluded an alliance with the Southern Song Dynasty against the Jin. The Southern Song rulers, ethnic Chinese who had been defeated by the Jurchens in 1127, were happy to help the Mongols deal with their old enemies, but their policy was a foolish one in the long run. After the Jin Dynasty was finally overthrown in 1234

Chinese painting showing a mounted Mongol archer.   Victoria and Albert Museum

by Genghis Khan's son Ögödei, it would be the turn of the Southern Song to try to fend off the conquering Mongols.

Genghis Khan next turned his attention to the west. In 1209, he had obtained the submission of the Uighur Turks of Turfan, an outpost in China's Xinjiang region, and from 1210 a Mongol garrison was stationed there. After the successful siege of Beijing, Turfan was used to

Yelu Qucai

We know him by his Chinese name, Yelu Qucai. His name in his own Khitan language must have been pronounced something like that (Yeah-loo choo-tsai), but we don't know for sure what it was. He was born around 1190, a descendant of the Khitan lords who had ruled in North China as the Liao Dynasty until the beginning of that century. His family had lived in China for generations, and he was raised as both a devout Buddhist and a Confucian gentleman-scholar. When he was first captured by the Mongols in 1215, he was listed as an astrologer and a sage.

Tall, handsome, and dignified, the young Yelu Qucai caught the eye of Genghis Khan, who quickly learned to trust his advice. He repeated to the Great Khan an old Chinese proverb: China can be conquered on horseback, but it cannot be ruled from horseback. More than anyone else, he taught Genghis Khan about the art of administration. As the great conquerer lay dying in 1227, he advised his son and successor Ögödei to listen to Yelu Qucai's advice.

Yelu Qucai soon proved his worth by persuading Ögödei not to stage a campaign against the Kara-Khitai kingdom of Turkestan. This kingdom was by then ruled not by Khitans, but by Genghis Khan's old Mongol enemies, the Naimans. In 1218, one of the best of the Mongol generals, Jebei, marched against the Naimans and, aided by an uprising of the local people, crushed them in battle. The Naiman king was hunted down and killed. Just to the west of Kara-Khitai was the Moslem

---

turn the agricultural lands of North China into pastures for Mongol horses. Instead, he set up a regular system of taxation that greatly increased the wealth of the Mongol Empire. His advice was not always heeded, however. His proposal to set up a system to recruit civil servants by competitive examinations, on the Chinese model, was rejected. And in 1239, Ögödei abandoned his orderly method of taxation in favor of using private tax agents who squeezed as much as they could out of the suffering peasants, kept a percentage for themselves, and sent the rest on to the Great Khan. (Some scholars have suggested that Ögödei craftily preferred this system of tax collection, which used mostly foreign Moslems as tax agents, because it deflected resentment away from the Mongols themselves.)

Yelu Qucai did succeed in persuading Ögödei that a great empire needed a great capital; Ögödei's response was to found the city of Karakorum on the Mongol steppe. His Khitan advisor played an important role in finding Chinese architects for its palaces, and in recruiting merchants to supply its markets.

A true Confucian gentleman, Yelu Qucai did not use the power of his position to become rich. When he died in 1243, he left his family only a library, some musical instruments, and a cabinet of herbal medicines.

kingdom of Khwarazm-shah Mohammed, who had recently taken over some of the Kara-Khitai lands and established a capital at Samarkand. In 1218, a Khwarazmid* regional governor attacked and massacred a caravan of Moslem merchants carrying Mongol goods. Three Mongol ambassadors were sent to demand an apology; one was killed, and the other two badly insulted. The only possible Mongol response was war.

In 1219, Genghis Khan himself headed a Mongol army of 150,000 riders in an attack on Khwarazm-shah's kingdom. The army advanced in a three-pronged formation, each column headed by one of Genghis Khan's sons. The Khwarazmid forces were quickly overwhelmed, and Khwarazm-shah Mohammed was pursued to the Caspian Sea; taking refuge on an island there, he was captured and killed. A more dangerous Khwarazmid prince, Jalal ad-Din, survived. Mongol armies pursued him, leaving great destruction in their wake, through Afghanistan to the banks of the Indus River. There Jalal ad-Din miraculously escaped once again, leaping from a cliff into the river, astride his horse. For years thereafter, he led his depleted forces in battle against the Mongols in various parts of the Middle East.

Ghengis Khan took vengeance for his murdered ambassador by slaughtering huge numbers of people in the Khwarazmid kingdom, leveling whole cities and destroying their vital irrigation works. His son Tolui spent the next several years destroying the western Khwarazmid provinces—the Khorasan region, in northeastern Iran and western Afghanistan—with even greater thoroughness. Oasis cities such as Ghazni, Balkh, Merv, and Herat, which had for centuries been centers of wealth and luxury astride the Silk Route, were reduced to rubble,

*The suffix "-id," here and elsewhere, means "pertaining to." Thus the word "Khwarazmid" means "having to do with the kingdom of Khwarazm-shah Mohammed," and "Genghisid" means "having to do with Genghis Khan."

their people slaughtered by the tens of thousands. (See *The Land and People of Afghanistan.*)

The Mongols moved on to the Caucasus. They briefly allied themselves with their cousins, the Kipchak Turks—also "people of the felt tents"—to defeat the Circassians of the Crimea. With the completion of that campaign, the Mongols then turned on the Kipchaks, and slaughtered them (along with their Russian allies) beneath the city walls of Kiev.

Surrender or Die

The campaigns of this period show the extent to which the Mongols had learned the art of large-scale warfare. They fought with huge, highly disciplined armies, controlling them in extended formations throughout long campaigns. The Mongol forces by this time included not only Mongols, but also contingents of their many allies and vassals, including Turks, Khitans, Chinese, and Tibetans. These extra troops included specialized units for siegecraft, transport, and territorial occupation.

Genghis Khan had also learned the use of terror as a military weapon. When his army arrived at the walls of a city, he did not usually attack immediately, but instead gave the inhabitants a choice: surrender or die. The price of surrender was high: If the city dwellers opened their gates to the Mongols, the victors would ride off with food, treasure, slaves, and any other spoils that they wanted; on the other hand, they would refrain from destroying the city or harming the people who remained in it. But the price of resistance was even higher: If the city gates were closed and the people fought back against the attackers, the Mongols, after their almost inevitable victory, would kill every living thing within the city walls. Moreover, before attacking they would often round up local people from the surrounding countryside and march them toward

the city in front of their own army, so that if the defenders fired at the Mongols, they would kill their own countrymen first. Word of these tactics quickly spread, and more and more cities chose to surrender without a fight.

After five years of strenuous campaigning in the west, Genghis Khan decided that it was time to return to Mongolia again. In 1223, he led his army home, but by a roundabout route, making a sweeping passage south of the Caspian Sea, then north along its western shore, and back east again through southern Russia. This was more of an exploratory mission than a campaign of conquest, although of course the army pillaged to supply its needs along the way; the intelligence gathered on this trip would be put to good use a few years later, when the Mongols invaded Russia and eastern Europe. Genghis Khan's army took the Russians completely by surprise. A Russian chronicle records, for the year 1224, that "For our sins, unknown tribes came, whom no one exactly knows, who they are, nor whence they came out, nor what their faith is; but they call them Tartars." Within a few years, the Russians would learn more than they wanted to know about these "unknown tribes."

Not all the Mongols returned eastward; an occupying force remained behind, south of the Aral Sea, under Jochi, the eldest son of Genghis Khan. Jochi, resentful at having been given what he considered a minor role in the warfare of the previous years, and at not being designated his father's heir apparent, was in a rebellious mood. Had he lived long, a civil war with his brothers might have broken out. But Jochi died in 1227, shortly before his father's death; his son Batu would inherit the western portion of the Mongol Empire.

Genghis Khan, in a posthumous and idealized portrait by an unknown Chinese artist.
National Palace Museum, Taipei, Taiwan, Republic of China

Back in Mongolia, Genghis Khan's first priority was to complete the destruction of the Xixia Kingdom, which had stubbornly held out against the Mongols since they first invaded it in 1207. In 1226 the Mongols invaded again in full force, and besieged the Xixia capital. The following year, taking a break from the campaign, Genghis Khan went hunting and had an accident; he fell heavily from his horse and was severely injured. The Xixia king offered to surrender, but as Genghis Khan lay dying, he showed no mercy to his old enemy, and had him killed. And then he issued a terrible final decree, ordering the total destruction of the Xixia Kingdom: "As long as I can eat food and still say, 'Make everyone who lives in their cities vanish,' kill them all and destroy their homes. As long as I am still alive, keep up the slaughter."

On August 18, 1227, Genghis Khan died. His body was placed in a yurt mounted on a huge oxcart, and carried secretly back to Mongolia. As a sacrifice to the soul of the fallen leader, Genghis Khan's bodyguards killed every person and animal encountered by the funeral procession in its journey of hundreds of miles. The Great Khan was placed in a hidden mountain grave near the source of the Onon River, not far from his birthplace. His body has never been found.

The Rise and Fall of the Mongol Empire

By the time of his death at age sixty-five, Genghis Khan had fully earned his title as the greatest conqueror in history. But the task of expanding the Mongol Empire to its fullest extent and of consolidating its government fell to his sons and, especially, his grandsons. These men established the Mongols firmly in power as rulers of most of the known world. At the same time, by gradually focusing their attention on the great civilizations they had conquered, to the neglect of their homeland in the steppe, they planted the seeds of the empire's disintegration.

The Great Khans

At the great *quriltai* that was held after the death of Genghis Khan, his third son, Ögödei, was elected his successor as Great Khan. In accordance with Genghis Khan's wishes, Jochi's son Batu was granted authority over the western part of the empire, Chagatai received the lands of Turkestan and Trans-Oxania, and Tolui was given control of China and the eastern empire (see genealogical table p. 79). As long as each of them acknowledged the authority of the Great Khan, the empire would retain some overall unity despite this division of responsibility; but the conflicts that would lead to disintegration had already begun.

Ögödei proved himself to be a worthy successor to Genghis Khan. He was capable of both ferocity and generosity; personally he was genial and warm-hearted, and perhaps overly fond of women and wine. Unlike his father, he loved luxury. Genghis Khan slept in yurts for his entire life; Ögödei brought architects, artisans, and merchants from China and elsewhere throughout the empire to build a grand capital city for the Great Khan at Karakorum, in the central Khangai steppe. He also had a greater interest in, and talent for, administration; building on his father's work, Ögödei systematized the application of the *yasa*, extended the "pony express" messenger system throughout the empire, and organized the constant flow of supplies by oxcart and caravan that was needed to support his capital city.

Ögödei was also a great conquerer in his own right. He completed the conquest of North China, besieging and capturing the Jin Dynasty's southern capital at Kaifeng in 1234. His father's old advisor, Yelu Qucai, saved the lives of the city's nearly 2 million inhabitants by persuading Ögödei to collect their taxes rather than their heads. In the same year, he consolidated Mongolian control of southern Manchuria, and pressed on to attack Korea; the Korean Koryŏ Dynasty capitulated in 1238.

Ögödei also turned his attention to the western empire. In 1237 he sent a huge force under the command of four grandsons of Genghis

Genghis Khan and his descendants.

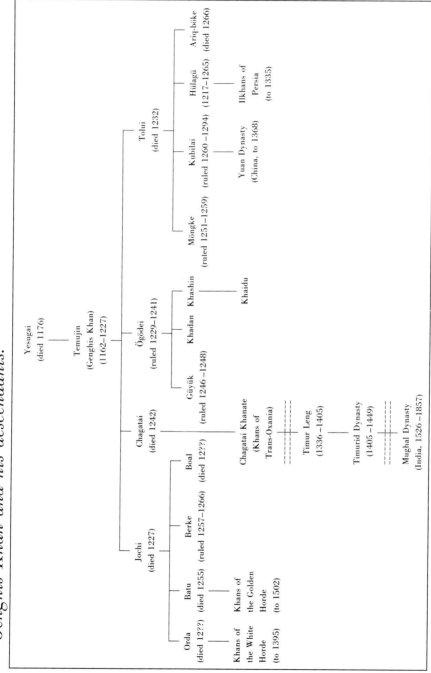

Khan, augmented by over a hundred thousand Turkish, Persian, Chinese, and other troops, to complete the work begun in Genghis Khan's sweep around the Caspian Sea in 1223–1224. The four commanders—Batu, son of Jochi; Büri, son of Chagatai; Möngke, son of Tolui; and Güyük, son of Ögödei—were rivals as much as comrades-in-arms, but despite their rivalries, the campaign was a spectacular success. The armies pressed straight westward from Mongolia, passing north of Lake Balkash, the Aral Sea, and the Caspian Sea. By early 1238 Batu had crossed the Volga and occupied Moscow; Kiev fell in December of the

The Mongol Impact on Europe

The Mongol invasion left a deep and lasting impression on the minds of Europeans, who thought that the Mongols were more fierce and terrible than any people they had ever encountered before. The thirteenth-century English historian Matthew Paris lived hundreds of miles away from the scenes of fighting in Poland and Hungary, but his account of the invasions reflects his horror at the eyewitness stories he had heard.

Swarming like locusts over the face of the earth, they have brought terrible devastation to the eastern parts of Europe laying it waste with fire and carnage. After having passed through the lands of the Saracens, they have razed cities, cut down forests, overthrown fortresses, pulled up vines, destroyed gardens, killed townspeople and peasants. If perchance they have spared any suppliants, they have forced them, reduced to the lower condition of slavery, to fight in the foremost ranks against their own neighbours. Those who have feigned to fight, or have hidden in the hope of escaping, have been followed up by the Tartars

same year. Having conquered Russia, the Mongol army pressed on into eastern Europe. In early 1241 they attacked Poland; after one savage battle they collected a cartload of ears sliced from the heads of their captives. Next they turned south to Hungary, capturing Buda and Pesth (modern Budapest) by the end of 1241.

The Mongols seemed invincible; the Europeans were totally unprepared to counter the Mongol tactics, which combined lightning campaigns through the countryside and devastating sieges of cities. The Holy Roman Empire of central Europe and the Byzantine Empire of the

---

and butchered. . . . For they are inhuman and beastly, rather monsters than men, thirsting for and drinking blood, tearing and devouring flesh of dogs and men, dressed in ox-hides, armed with plates of iron, short and stout, thickset, strong, invincible, indefatigable, their backs unprotected, their breast covered with armour: drinking with delight the pure blood of their flocks, with big, strong horses, which eat branches and even trees. . . . They are without human laws, know no comforts, are more ferocious than lions or bears. . . . They have one-edged swords and daggers, are wonderful archers, spare neither age, nor sex, nor condition. They know no other language than their own, which no one else knows; for until now there has been no access to them, nor did they go forth from their own country; so there could be no knowledge of their customs or persons. . . . They wander about with their flocks and their wives, who are taught to fight like men. And so they came with the swiftness of lightning to the confines of Christendom, ravaging and slaughtering, striking everyone with terror and incomparable horror.

J. A. Giles, trans., *Matthew Paris' English History*, Vol. 1 (London, 1852), pp. 312–313.

eastern Mediterranean were probably saved from Mongol conquest only by a lucky accident: the death of Ögödei in December 1241. The Mongol commanders, informed of the Great Khan's death by fast messengers from the steppe, withdrew their forces into Russia and hurried back to Karakorum for the *quriltai* that would choose Ögödei's successor. By the time Batu arrived, it was clear that he would be passed over in the succession. Ögödei's son Güyük, promoted by his strong-willed and politically astute mother, was to be the next Great Khan. At the *quriltai* Batu reluctantly agreed to his cousin's election, and then went back to Russia to rule over the lands of his Golden Horde. He died in Russia in 1255.

Güyük was a sullen and morose man who was content to spend most of his reign in the royal city of Karakorum. His still-simmering rivalry with Batu prevented the kind of cooperation that might have renewed the thrust of Mongol conquest in the west. His reign was, however, notable for the beginning of diplomatic contacts between Europe and the Mongol Empire. In 1245 two Franciscan friars, Giovanni Carpini and Benedict of Poland, visited Karakorum as papal emissaries, and reported back to Rome on the splendor of the Mongol capital and the strength of the Mongol armies. Over the next few decades, a steady stream of European ambassadors, including such famous figures as William of Rubruck, Odoric of Pordenone, and John of Montecorvino, would visit Karakorum, while Mongol ambassadors were dispatched to Rome, Paris, and even as far as England. The Europeans had two aims: first, to gauge the strength of the Mongols and the likelihood that they would try again to conquer Europe, and second, to form an alliance with the Mongols to aid the Christian Crusades against the Moslem rulers of Palestine. The Mongols, for their part, were interested in weighing the possible advantages of cooperation with the Crusaders, but mainly they were satisfied to see the ambassadors of European kings and popes

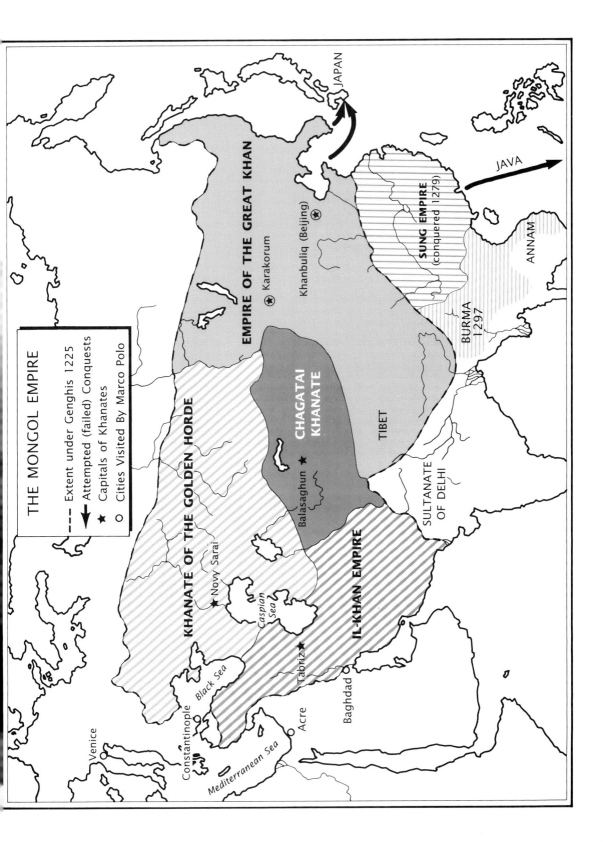

THE MONGOL EMPIRE

- – – – Extent under Genghis 1225
- ⟶ Attempted (failed) Conquests
- ★ Capitals of Khanates
- ○ Cities Visited By Marco Polo

EMPIRE OF THE GREAT KHAN

⊛ Karakorum

Khanbuliq (Beijing) ⊛

SUNG EMPIRE
(conquered 1279)

JAPAN

JAVA

ANNAM

BURMA
1297

TIBET

**CHAGATAI
KHANATE**

KHANATE OF THE GOLDEN HORDE

★ Balasaghun

**SULTANATE
OF DELHI**

★ Novy Sarai

IL-KHAN EMPIRE

Caspian
Sea

★ Tabriz

○ Baghdad

Black Sea

○ Constantinople

○ Acre

○ Venice

Mediterranean Sea

arrive to pay tribute, as they saw it, to the rulers of most of the world.

The Mongol Empire, by the reign of Güyük, included people of many religious faiths: animists, Buddhists, Zoroastrians, Nestorian and Eastern Orthodox Christians, and others. All those religions were tolerated equally; the Mongols had no wish to pursue religious politics within their empire. Islam, however, was another matter. The Mongols were

Rashid al-Din

One of the best sources of information on the history of the Mongol Empire is the work of Rashid al-Din (1247–1318), who is still famous in the Islamic world as one of the greatest historians of all time. A Jewish convert to Islam, Rashid was trained as a physician, but soon abandoned the practice of medicine to become a political advisor to the Ilkhan Abagha of Persia. Under the Ilkhan Ghazan he rose to the office of Grand Vizier, chief administrator of the vast Persian empire of the Mongols. In addition to his work as a statesman, he was a prolific writer and an accomplished theologian. At Ghazan's request, he wrote a history of the Mongol Empire from its origins to his own time. That work, the *Ta'rikh-i Ghazani,* was later expanded during the reign of Öljeitü to become a history of the entire known world.

Rashid was a conscientious historian, and he recorded in great detail the administrative and economic history of the empire as well as its military campaigns. The *Ta'rikh-i Gazani* is full, as one might expect, of pillage and slaughter, but Rashid also tried hard (perhaps out of loyalty to his sovereigns) to portray the Mongol leaders as real people, capable of humor and compassion as well as of ferocity. The following story, paraphrased from Rashid's history of the

well aware of the militant intolerance toward pagans in the Moslem world, where church and state were one. In the mid-thirteenth century they began to plan their conquest of the Middle East.

Güyük died suddenly in 1248, and another *quriltai* was convened. Batu let it be known that he favored the election of his cousin Möngke, Tolui's eldest son, but stubbornly refused to leave his stronghold on the

Mongols, is typical of his efforts to show the human side of the Great Khans:

According to the yasa, *it is forbidden for anyone to bathe or wash clothes in running water. One day some Mongol guardsmen saw a Moslem bathing in a stream; they seized him and brought him before the Great Khan Ögödei for sentencing. But the Great Khan felt sorry for the man, condemned by a law of which he was ignorant. Speaking to the Moslem in private, the Great Khan told him to plead that he was a pauper and, having accidentally dropped his last piece of silver into the stream, he waded in to find it. Then the Great Khan secretly sent one of his servants to throw a piece of silver into the stream.*

The next morning, the case was heard in court. The Moslem told the story as the Great Khan had instructed him. The Great Khan then sent his guards to the stream to see if they could find evidence that the man was telling the truth. When they returned with the piece of silver, the Great Khan pardoned the Moslem for violating the yasa, *and sent him away with a reward of ten additional pieces of silver for his trouble.*

Rashid al-Din himself learned, however, that Mongol justice could be cruel. When the Ilkhan Öljeitü died, his son Abu Sa'id accused Rashid of having poisoned him, and Rashid was put to death.

Volga to participate in the election. This created a stalemate; no Great Khan could be elected without the direct participation of all of Genghis Khan's descendants. Finally, in 1251, Möngke took Batu's continued absence as a sign of agreement, and mounted the throne at Karakorum. Möngke brought a renewed vigor to the Mongol leadership, and expressed that vigor by the resumption of conquest.

Möngke dispatched his brother Kubilai to China to oversee the empire there, and to renew the Mongol campaigns against the Southern Song Dynasty. Kubilai's first assignment was to conquer the independent Chinese kingdom of Dali, in Yunnan Province along the route to Burma. Leading his army south through western China in 1253, Kubilai and his trusted general Bayan arrived at the Jinsha River and found the Dali army waiting on the opposite bank. After making a daring nighttime crossing of the river on inflated skin rafts, the Mongols slaughtered their astonished opponents and sent the survivors fleeing back to their capital, which later surrendered without a fight. Over the next four years Kubilai's forces extended their control in southwestern China, pushing also into eastern Tibet, and even briefly occupying Hanoi in 1257. While his armies campaigned in the south, Kubilai concentrated on learning the techniques of Chinese bureaucratic administration to govern the vast territory under his control. He established his own capital city at Shangdu, north of Beijing on the border between China and Mongolia, and began to assemble advisors and administrators from all over the empire: Chinese, Turks, Persians, Nestorian Christians from Sogdia, and many others. Much later, their ranks would include even an adventurous Venetian merchant, Marco Polo. Kubilai's days of glory lay in the future, however. In 1258, Möngke, complaining that his brother was becoming "too Chinese," summoned him back to Mongolia; Kubilai complied, knowing that his position in China was secure.

In 1256, Möngke sent another of his brothers, Hülegü, to conquer the Moslem lands of the Middle East. Hülegü carried out his mission

Persian miniature painting showing Hülegü's siege of Baghdad in 1258. Bibliothèque Nationale, Paris

with spectacular success. In 1257 he besieged the fortress of the Islamic Isma'ili Order (popularly known as the Assassins) in the Elburz Mountains of northern Iran, and, after its surrender, had all of its defenders slaughtered. The following year he pressed on to Baghdad, capital of the Abassid Empire of Persia. After taking that city, he allowed his troops to sack it at will while he executed the caliph, the ruler of the Abassid Empire and acknowledged leader of most of the Moslem world. With Baghdad destroyed, Hülegü founded his own dynasty, the Ilkhanate of Persia; he shifted the capital from Baghdad to Tabriz, nearer to the steppelands of Central Asia.

Hülegü next moved on into Syria and Palestine, thrusting toward Egypt, when word arrived that Möngke had died. He withdrew his forces to Azerbaijan, leaving behind only a skeleton occupying army in Syria. Hülegü traveled back to Mongolia to participate in the election of the next Great Khan—a complex and bitterly contested political struggle that absorbed all of his attention. As Europe was saved by the death of Ögödei, Egypt was saved by the death of Möngke. When Syrian spies reported to the Mameluke rulers of Egypt that most of the Mongols had departed, a Mameluke army was dispatched to Palestine to deal with the Mongol garrison. Ambushed at Ain Jalyut, north of Jerusalem, on September 3, 1260, the vastly outnumbered Mongols were dealt a crushing defeat that marked the end of the empire's expansion in the west.

The Empire Divides

The *quriltai* of 1260 resulted in Kubilai's election as Great Khan, but the election was not regarded as valid by all of his kinsmen, and it marked the end of even nominal unity within the Mongol Empire. For the first time, a *quriltai* had been held not in Mongolia, but in China; Kubilai feared the rising power of his younger brother Ariq-böke, and preferred to have himself elected Great Khan in the safety of his own domain. Ariq-böke responded by convening a *quriltai* of his own supporters in Mongolia, and proclaimed himself Great Khan as well. The dispute went to the brink of open warfare before Ariq-böke yielded to his more powerful elder brother in 1264. Ariq-böke conveniently died in 1266; some say he was poisoned. Kubilai's election was upheld, but his real authority never extended much beyond China. Möngke was right: Kubilai had indeed become "too Chinese," and although he was the legal ruler of Mongolia, he spent the rest of his life conquering and governing China. In 1260 he announced that he was taking the title of Emperor of China as the founder of the Yuan Dynasty; he showed little interest in trying to assert his authority over the western parts of the empire. For their part, the rulers of the Golden Horde and the Ilkhanate of Persia gave only grudging consent to Kubilai's election, and had no intention of allowing him to interfere in their domains. The Khanate of Chagatai's descendants in Turkestan was secure but also rather passive; the Chagatid Khans played little further role in Mongol imperial affairs until the waning days of Mongol power, far in the future.

In the west, Mongol rivalries soon broke out into open warfare. Batu had died in 1255, to be succeeded as leader of the Golden Horde by his short-lived son and grandson. In 1257 Batu's brother Berke inherited the Golden Horde, and became also the first important Mongol leader to convert to Islam. The armies of the Golden Horde by that time included as many Turks as Mongols, and its subjects were Turks, Russians, and various peoples of the Caucasus. In 1262 Berke formed an alliance with the Mamelukes of Egypt against Hülegü's Ilkhanate of Persia, and fought the first of many wars between those two divisions of the Mongol Empire. The issue was partly one of religion, but more important was the question of which Mongol dynasty would control the rich agricultural lands of Azerbaijan. Meanwhile, another of Batu's sons, Orda, split from the Golden Horde to establish his own obscure domain, the independent Khanate of the White Horde east of the Ural Mountains.

None of Berke's immediate successors became Moslems; the religious issue in the Golden Horde remained unsettled until Özbeg, who reigned from 1313 to 1341, declared Islam the official religion of his Khanate. In the Ilkhanate, Hülegü converted to Lamaistic Buddhism late in his life, and that faith was followed by his successors until Ghazan Khan converted to Islam in 1295. Thereafter, the Mongol rulers of the Golden Horde in southern Russia, and the Ilkhanate in greater Persia, tended gradually to lose their own ethnic identity. In literature and the arts, as well as in religion, the western realms of the Mongol Empire quickly became more Middle Eastern than Mongolian.

Kubilai Khan and the Yuan Dynasty

The Mongol appetite for conquest persisted only in Kubilai's own domain. Kubilai essentially abandoned Karakorum and spent almost all his life in China, dividing his time between Shangdu and a new capital at Dadu, built on the ruins of the Jin capital at Beijing. The Southern Song emperor unwisely launched attacks on Kubilai's forces in 1261 and 1262; Kubilai's counterattack in 1264 crushed the Song forces in Sichuan Province and left Kubilai in command of a fleet of river boats. As Genghis Khan had had to learn siege warfare in his early campaigns against China, so now did Kubilai have to learn the techniques of naval warfare. Southern China is dominated by rivers and canals, mountains and rice paddies—unfamiliar and difficult terrain for Mongol horsemen. Over the next decade, Kubilai's forces, under the command of his great general Bayan, learned to fight from ships, defending themselves against Song gunpowder rockets and flamethrowers, and then using them themselves. After ten years of nearly continuous warfare, Bayan crossed the Yangtse River at Hankou in January 1275, and was at the walls of the Southern Song capital at Hangzhou in December of that same year. He had defeated Chinese armies time and again while fighting his way down the Yangtse; Chinese battle losses mounted into the hundreds of thousands. In 1276 Hangzhou surrendered, but the Song emperor fled southward, and Song loyalists fought on in other walled cities, compelling the Mongols to take all of southern China by force. Finally, in a great naval battle early in 1279, the ship carrying the last Song emperor—a young boy—was sunk, and the dynasty came to an end.

Kubilai, in 1279, was the undisputed master of East Asia; his Yuan Dynasty ruled all of China, and dominated Manchuria and Korea to the east. His ambitions did not stop there, however. He wished also to be regarded as truly Great Khan of all the Mongols, on the one hand, and to conquer even more of East Asia, on the other. His attempts to be recognized as the supreme ruler of the Mongol Empire were largely frustrated; the Golden Horde and the Ilkhanate of Persia were entirely outside his control, and the Chagatid Khanate of Turkestan was nearly so. In western Mongolia and the Central Asian hinterlands of China, he was forced to use both warfare and diplomacy to assert his power against his brother Ariq-böke, Ögödei's grandson Khaidu, and other rivals for power. Kubilai prevailed against them, but his control was never entirely secure. Nevertheless, he succeeded in his principal aims of keeping Mongolia itself loyal to his rule, and in controlling the caravan routes between China and western Asia.

The artist who painted this scene (from Le Livre des Merveilles, *about 1350) imagined Kubilai Khan dressed as a medieval nobleman in a European setting, hunting with a trained cheetah and a falcon.* Bibliothèque Nationale, Paris

Farther east, in 1274 and again in 1281, Kubilai pressured his Korean vassals to aid in forming huge fleets to transport invading Mongol armies to Japan. On both occasions the Mongols succeeded in reaching the shores of Japan's Kyushu Island and establishing beachheads; on both occasions, typhoons destroyed the Mongol fleets offshore, leaving the invaders to be cut down by samurai arrows. The

Marco Polo

Marco Polo was born in Venice around 1254. In 1260, his father and uncle went on a trading journey to the Caucasus; finding their homeward route blocked by warfare (both Batu and Hülegü had armies in the field), they continued on to China, reaching Kaifeng in 1266. In 1269, they returned to Venice, and two years later set out again, taking Marco with them. They arrived in Kubilai Khan's capital in 1275. Marco's father, Niccolo, and his uncle, Matteo, apparently continued their careers as merchants in China, but young Marco himself quickly became a favorite of the Great Khan, and joined his imperial government. Kubilai Khan, like his grandfather, was good at recognizing talent when he saw it, and had a policy of employing foreigners in his administration.

For seventeen years Marco served Kubilai Khan as a kind of roving inspector of the empire; he traveled widely throughout China and as far as Burma, reporting back to the Great Khan whenever he returned to the capital. He must have learned to speak both Mongolian and Chinese to some extent, but he never learned to read or write Chinese, and never formed any close ties

Japanese, giving thanks to the Buddha for their salvation, hailed the typhoons as *kamikaze*, "divine winds"—a term that would be used again for the Japanese suicide dive-bomber squadrons at the end of World War II. Between 1283 and 1288, Kubilai launched several attacks by both land and sea against Annam and Champa, two kingdoms in what is now Vietnam; both were brought under loose Mongol control.

with the elite Chinese bureaucracy.

The Venetians left China in 1292 by sea, escorting a wife of the Ilkhan of Persia back to Baghdad. They arrived home in Venice in 1295. Marco Polo joined the Venetian armed forces fighting a war with Genoa in 1296, and promptly was taken prisoner. While in captivity, he dictated (in French) an account of his life to a fellow prisoner. *The Book of Marco Polo* is a detailed memoir of his travels to and throughout China; in it he was careful to distinguish between what he saw and what he only heard about. It is clear that he exaggerated to some extent, and misunderstood some of what he saw, but on the whole the book is remarkably accurate.

His contemporaries found it all very hard to believe, however; Marco Polo became popularly known as "Marco of the Thousand Lies." But even those who did not believe were fascinated by what he said. For over three hundred years Marco Polo's book was almost the only source of information on China available in Europe. Its picture of "Cathay"—China—as a land of fabulous riches inspired many other adventurers to try to go and see for themselves; it was one of the most important inspirations of the European Age of Exploration in the fifteenth century.

The Juyang Gate in the Great Wall of China, north of Beijing. This gate was built by Kubilai Khan as a symbolic passageway linking Mongolia and China; it pierces the wall that had formerly divided the two territories.

His successor, Timur Öljeitü, extended Mongol dominion even farther into Southeast Asia, conquering parts of northern Laos, Thailand, Burma, and eastern Assam.

Kubilai's last attempt at long-range maritime conquest was, like the Japanese ventures, a disaster. In 1289, a Mongol ambassador to Java had been seized, branded on the face, and sent home in disgrace. To avenge that insult Kubilai, in 1292, dispatched a fleet of a thousand ships to conquer Java. Meanwhile the offending king, Kertanagara, had been overthrown in a rebellion; the Mongol troops were met cordially by Kertanagara's son-in-law, who offered to join them in punishing the kingdom, now in rebel hands. The two armies joined in laying waste to

Kertanagara's old domain; resting from the battle, the Mongols were then set upon by their Javanese allies and slaughtered.

Though Kubilai ruled China as a conqueror, he ruled well. His dynasty governed through a traditional Chinese bureaucratic administration (see *The Land and People of China*) combined with an overlay of Mongol military occupation and non-Chinese administrators and advisors at the top of the bureaucratic ladder. Kubilai moved quickly to restore China from the ravages of decades of warfare; irrigation works were restored, a new branch of the Grand Canal was built to link the Yangtse River with Dadu (Beijing); hospitals were established, along with a new system of assistance to the poor. Kubilai was a patron of science and the arts. In the 1280's the Royal Astronomer Guo Shoujing built what was then the world's best astronomical observatory near Kubilai's royal palace at Dadu. The Yuan Dynasty produced some of China's greatest painters, and the art of blue-and-white porcelain reached new heights. Literature, and especially theater, flourished.

The later emperors of the Yuan Dynasty, however, lacked Kubilai Khan's energy, wisdom, and sense of vision. By the 1330's, the Chinese

A Vision of Cathay

Marco Polo's account of "Cathay" during the reign of Kubilai Khan struck most Europeans at the time as outlandish and unbelievable. But it planted, nevertheless, a long-lasting vision of Cathay as a land of mystery and splendor, a land more of legend than of reality. Six centuries after Kubilai came to the throne of China, Samuel Taylor Coleridge captured the magical memory of the Khan's imperial capital in Xanadu (Shangdu) in his most famous poem:

Kubla Khan

In Xanadu did Kubla Khan
A stately pleasure-dome decree:
Where Alph, the sacred river, ran
Through caverns measureless to man
Down to a sunless sea.
So twice five miles of fertile ground
With walls and towers were girdled round:
And there were gardens bright with sinuous rills
Where blossomed many an incense-bearing tree;
And here were forests ancient as the hills,
Enfolding sunny spots of greenery.
But oh, that deep romantic chasm which slanted
Down the green hill athwart a cedarn cover!
A savage place! as holy and enchanted
As e'er beneath a waning moon was haunted
By woman wailing for her demon-lover!
And from this chasm, with ceaseless turmoil
seething,
As if this earth in fast thick pants were
breathing,
A mighty fountain momently was forced:
Amid whose swift half-intermitted burst
Huge fragments vaulted like rebounding hail,
Or chaffy grain beneath the thresher's flail:
And 'mid these dancing rocks at once and ever
It flung up momently the sacred river.
Five miles meandering with a mazy motion
Through wood and dale the sacred river ran,

Then reached the caverns measureless to man,
And sank in tumult to a lifeless ocean:
And 'mid this tumult Kubla heard from far
Ancestral voices prophesying war!
The shadow of the dome of pleasure
Floated midway on the waves;
Where was heard the mingled measure
From the fountains and the caves.
It was a miracle of rare device,
A sunny pleasure-dome with caves of ice.
A damsel with a dulcimer
In a vision once I saw:
It was an Abyssinian maid,
And on her dulcimer she played,
Singing of Mount Abora.
Could I revive within me,
Her symphony and song,
To such a deep delight 'twould win me,
That with music loud and long,
I would build that dome in air,
That sunny dome! those caves of ice!
And all who heard should see them there,
And all should cry, Beware! Beware!
His flashing eyes, his floating hair!
Weave a circle round him thrice,
And close your eyes with holy dread,
For he on honey-dew hath fed,
And drunk the milk of Paradise.

population increasingly regarded their Mongol rulers, and especially the large and expensive garrisons of Mongol horsemen that they maintained throughout the country, as burdensome as well as foreign. The Chinese elite grew resentful at the Mongols' employment of foreigners at the upper reaches of government. Rebellions broke out with increasing frequency, culminating in the quasireligious anti-Mongol movement of Zhu Yuanzhang, an ex-Buddhist monk turned rebel general. In 1368 Zhu's army sacked and burned the Mongol palaces at Dadu, and then pressed on into Mongolia itself to burn Karakorum to rubble.

The End of the Empire

By the time the Yuan Dynasty fell, the Ilkhanate of Persia had already been extinct for thirty years. Abu Sa'id, the last Ilkhan, was a capable ruler; he patronized Persian art and literature, negotiated peace with the Mamelukes of Egypt, and ruled in tranquility. But he left no son, and on his death his empire dissolved into anarchy. Persia was left with no effective central rule until, at the end of the fourteenth century, it was briefly united once again by Timur Leng, the last of the great Mongol conquerors.

The Golden Horde lasted far longer, though its decline also began in the mid-fourteenth century. It revived briefly under Tokhtamish, who came to the throne of the Golden Horde in 1376; he united his territory with that of the White Horde to the east, and allied himself with Timur

This elaborately carved stucco mihrab *(a niche indicating the direction of Mecca, and therefore the direction toward which Moslems pray) was donated to the Friday Mosque in Isfahan, Persia, by the Ilkhan Öljeitü (ruled 1304–1316). Öljeitü personified the Mongol attitude of religious toleration; he himself was, at various times, a believer in shamanism, a Buddhist, a Nestorian Christian (taking the name Nicholas when he was baptized), a Sunni Moslem, and a Sufi.*

Leng. Yet Tokhtamish suffered the disgrace of being the first Mongol to be defeated in battle by the Russian Kingdom of Moscow, at Kulikovo Polye in 1380, an early sign that the balance of power in Russia was changing. Tokhtamish was overthrown and killed in 1395 by Timur Leng, his former patron and ally. The territory of the Golden Horde was split into four parts during the fifteenth century, and the destruction of the largest division, the "Great Horde," in a battle in the Crimea in 1502, is usually taken to mark the end of the Golden Horde's existence. A few remnants of the old empire endured beyond that, however; in 1552–1554 Kazan and Astrakhan fell to the armies of Ivan the Terrible, while the Tatar Crimean Horde remained independent but obscure until it was annexed by Russia under Catherine the Great in 1783.

The longest legacy of Mongol rule is found in the lineage of the Chagatid Khanate of Turkestan. The Chagatid Khans were overshadowed by their powerful relatives during the height of the Mongol Empire, but they had the advantage of ruling a territory that was culturally and geographically close to that of their Mongol homeland. They ruled without distinction throughout the fourteenth century, and then produced one final burst of Mongol conquest. Timur Leng (known in the west as Tamerlane) was born in Samarkand around 1336, of Mongol descent although not necessarily (as he claimed) of the lineage of Genghis Khan. Despite his ancestry, he was a Turkish-speaking Moslem with no real ties to Mongolia. In approximately 1370 he raised an army and gained effective control of the Chagatid Khanate; his armies then broke out from their base in Samarkand and spent the next thirty-five years in ceaseless campaigns that ranged through Afghanistan and Persia and as far as

A mounted Mongol ("Tatar") archer of the Golden Horde of southern Russia, as imagined by a sixteenth-century German wood-block artist. From Arthaud and Hébert-Stevens, *Mongolie*, after an unidentified print in the British Library

Palestine and Turkey; through the lands of the Golden Horde in southern Russia west to the Ukraine and the Black Sea; and south through the Khyber Pass as far as Delhi. After the battle of Delhi, Timur Leng made a pyramid of 80,000 heads hacked from the bodies of his defeated enemies. For sheer ferocity, his armies put even the forces of Genghis Khan to shame; one historian has called Timur Leng "the most comprehensively destructive monarch in history." Much of the Moslem world was despoiled to bring treasure back to Timur Leng's capital at Samarkand, which became for a while the most splendid city in Central Asia.

Timur Leng's empire collapsed almost immediately after his death in 1405, though his successors continued to govern the Chagatid Khanate from Samarkand, which they turned into a great center of Islamic art and learning. In 1523, however, Timur Leng's descendant Babur embarked on a new wave of conquest, through Afghanistan into India. With his victory at the Battle of Panipat in 1526 he established the Mughal Dynasty of India, which was to endure until 1857. Its name was a dim reminder of the glory of the Mongols.

The Mongol Legacy

The Mongol Empire is a classic example of the difficulty of establishing and maintaining an empire based on tribal rule. A tribal confederation, once assembled, must conquer and expand or else it will dissolve. Victory after victory is needed to reward the confederation's members. But victory creates new problems, as settled civilizations come under tribal rule, and must be administered in ways quite foreign to tribal society. In the case of the Mongol Empire, the establishment of control

Timur Leng on his throne in Samarkand. Although of Mongol descent, Timur Leng was culturally Turkish, as his clothing and weapons show. The Bettmann Archive

over southern Russia, Persia, and China led inevitably to a split in the empire, and to the establishment of separate Mongol monarchies ruling in the styles of their conquered territories. (Timur Leng provides an example of the other possibility: He pillaged but did not govern; his empire collapsed upon his death.) The result was a vacuum at the center. Mongolia remained of central importance to Genghis Khan and his sons, but by the time of his grandsons, it had become secondary to their own realms. The capital city of Karakorum was an extravagant exercise in Mongol imperial vanity. It was far too large, and too luxurious, to be supplied by its own Mongol hinterland, and required an endless stream of provisions brought expensively by oxcart and caravan from distant agricultural lands. Its virtual abandonment after the reign of Möngke was almost a matter of necessity.

Mongolia had become nearly a backwater even during the height of the Mongol Empire. In the far-flung reaches of the empire, the Mongol rulers were secure only as long as their military power and administrative talents could subdue their unwilling subjects. When the Golden Horde, the Ilkhanate, and the Yuan Dynasty fell, they disappeared with hardly a trace. Mongol culture had little impact on the peoples of the empire apart from the Turks, who in any case were themselves "dwellers in felt tents." Tribal peoples in Central Asia today trace their laws to Genghis Khan's *yasa*, but in the urban and agricultural lands of Russia, Iran, and China, the Mongols are remembered only as barbarians of unusual ferocity.

Nevertheless, the Mongol Empire did have an impact on world history during its brief century of glory. Despite the relentless bloodshed of the Mongol conquests, the thirteenth century is also known as the time of the Pax Mongolica, the "Mongol Peace," when the vast trans-Asian steppe belt and the civilizations adjoining it were united under a single rule. (The Mongols boasted that a young woman could walk across Asia carrying a pot of gold on her head without being molested.) This achievement allowed an exceptional flowering of trade, diplomacy, and other contact throughout Europe and Asia that had lasting consequences. Tales of travelers like Marco Polo, though half disbelieved, also gave Europeans a permanent lust for the treasures of the land they called Cathay. After the collapse of the Mongol Empire, trade continued to flow across Asia between Europe and China, but control of the caravan routes fell into the hands of various Arab, Persian, and Central Asian intermediaries. The urgent need to find a safer and less expensive route between Europe and China led directly to the fifteenth-century Portuguese voyages around Africa, and to Columbus's discovery of the New World. By opening briefly the door between Europe and easternmost Asia, the Mongol Empire helped to usher in the European Age of Exploration.

A Nation in Decline

After the Mongol Empire collapsed in the fourteenth century, Mongolia became, and remained for centuries, an obscure, remote, and sparsely inhabited land of the steppes. Despite occasional flashes of Mongol power, and the very significant development of Lamaistic Buddhism as a key element of Mongol culture, the history of Mongolia from the fourteenth century to the beginning of the twentieth century is largely one of decline. Not until the early decades of the twentieth century would Mongolia experience a national revival, driven by the forces of revolution.

The Ashes of Empire

The fall of the Mongol Yuan Dynasty of China brought about a fundamental realignment of tribal power in Mongolia. Although the Ming Dynasty that took over from the Mongols in China pursued the retreating Mongols far into the steppes and destroyed Karakorum, they did not succeed in establishing long-term Chinese control there. But they did smash the monopoly of power in Mongolia that had been held by the descendants of Genghis Khan. This allowed the Ming emperors to engage in the age-old Chinese foreign-policy game of playing off one "barbarian" people against another.

With the collapse of the Genghisid confederation, pan-Mongolian power became a thing of the past, and regional tribal groupings formed. The most powerful were a group of tribes collectively known as the Oirats, whose territory extended from western Mongolia into Chinese Turkestan and the borderlands of Tibet. The Oirat group included a number of separate tribes, such as the Dörvöds, the Jüngars (who gave their name to the part of China's Xinjiang Province known as Dzungaria), and the Torguts. In eastern Mongolia and the borderlands of Manchuria, a small tribal confederation owed allegiance to the descendants of Khasar, a brother of Genghis Khan. Between those eastern and western confederations lay the Buriats of the Lake Baikal region, the Khalkas of the Khangai steppe, and the Chakhars of the Gobi. These central tribes were united from 1470 to 1543 in a confederation founded by Dayan Khan, a descendant of Kubilai.

The leaders of the tribes had learned an important lesson from the era of the Mongol Empire: Long-term power on the steppes could not be achieved on the basis of tribal loyalties alone. Aristocratic rule (as opposed to tribal chieftainship) could be sustained over the course of generations only when control over the steppe was extended to include towns and cultivated fields in the Chinese borderlands. Governing settled populations allowed tribal leaders to store grain and other forms of wealth, and to purchase the services of artisans and merchants. This

new form of Mongol power posed a constant problem for the Ming Dynasty, which used military force, tribal politics, and sometimes the payment of "gifts" (bribes) to try to achieve peace and stability on China's northern border.

During the early Ming Dynasty the most significant Mongol power was the Oirat confederation. The Oirats employed Uighur, Tibetan, and other merchants, administrators, and artisans to solidify their control of areas where Ming power was never fully established. Later, another confederation arose in the Ordos, the great northern loop of the Yellow River, under Altan Khan, who ruled from 1543 to 1583. Altan's confederation did not survive his death, but he remains a crucial figure in Mongol history for having solidified the authority of Lamaism in Mongolia. Another descendant of Dayan Khan ruled with some success among the Chakhars of the Gobi from 1604 to 1634, but his attempt at establishing a durable confederation was abruptly halted by the rise of a new, non-Mongol, tribal group in the northeast: the Manchus.

Lamaism

As rulers of China, the Mongols of the Yuan Dynasty became familiar with various forms of Buddhism. The long-standing cultural ties between Mongolia and Tibet led the Yuan aristocracy to favor the Lamaistic form of Buddhism that had developed in Tibet (see Chapter VI), and Lamaism gained a foothold in China and various other parts of the

Two Mongol women of the Oirat tribe near the northern border of Inner Mongolia, 1925. Their shabby clothing reflects the poverty of the lives of ordinary people at the time of the Mongolian Revolution; their elaborate silver headdresses display their tribal affiliation, and also contain much of their family wealth in a compact and portable form. Neg. no. 265399 (Photo by Shackelford), Courtesy Department of Library Services, American Museum of Natural History.

Mongol monks (lamas) at the Yonghuogong Temple, Beijing, late nineteenth century. They are wearing formal clerical dress, including the distinctive headgear of the Tibetan Yellow Hat Sect of Lamaism. Lamaistic temples dominated Mongolian society throughout the Mongolian culture area (even extending into northern China) in prerevolutionary times. Neg. no. 336452, Courtesy Department of Library Services, American Museum of Natural History

Mongol Empire during the late thirteenth century. The true establishment of Lamaism as a central force in Mongolian culture and society came later, however, during the reign of Altan Khan. Moved in part by genuine religious interest, but also mindful of the advantages of strengthening ties between Tibet and Mongolia, Altan Khan invited to the Ordos an important Tibetan lama and bestowed upon him the Mongolian title "Dalai" (meaning "all-encompassing"). Thus the principal lineage of the Tibetan clergy was established by a Mongol Khan. Following this, Lamaistic temples in Mongolia grew in wealth and power, and they imported religious texts, sacred paintings *(tanka)* and other religious implements, and large numbers of monks from Tibet itself. The chief Mongolian temples came to be headed by "Living Buddhas," reincarnations of important Tibetan lamas. Conveniently, the first Mongol reincarnation of the Living Buddha of Urga (now Ulan Bator) was found to be a descendant of the Genghisid khans of the Khalka tribe, thus uniting secular and spiritual power in central Mongolia.

The power of the Lamaistic temples grew rapidly, as pious donations gave them ever-increasing wealth, control of grazing lands, and even labor, for it became customary for every Mongol family to donate one son to be raised in a temple to pursue a career as a monk, and a smaller number of women became nuns. Lamaism encouraged the cultivation of deep religious faith among the Mongols, and also enriched the development of Mongolian art and literature. It also was a drain on the country's wealth and productivity, probably weakening Mongolia militarily and retarding its economy. With the Manchu conquest of Mongolia, however, Lamaism provided one anchor of cultural stability in an otherwise chaotic and disastrous period.

Mongolia Under Manchu Rule

The first stirrings of Manchu power were felt around the end of the fifteenth century. For several generations Manchu tribal leaders built a confederation (including some eastern Mongolian tribes) that rose to

Ma Zhang Chasing the Enemy, *a painting by the Jesuit missionary Guiseppe Castiglione, who became a court artist to the Chinese emperor in the eighteenth century. The rulers of China's Qing Dynasty were originally nomads from Manchuria; they adopted the typical cavalry techniques of the steppe tribes.* National Palace Museum, Taipei, Taiwan, Republic of China

power in Manchuria, drawing wealth and even political support from Chinese cities and agricultural communities beyond the Great Wall. By 1618, the Manchus had threatened Korea, and had begun to establish a rear base in the borderlands between the Mongolian steppes and the Great Wall. (The distinction between "Inner Mongolia"—that is, the portion of Mongolia near China—and "Outer Mongolia" dates from this time.) By 1629, the Manchus, under their great leader Nurhachi, were inside the Wall, and in 1637 they invaded Korea. In 1644 a rebel movement against the Ming Dynasty (which by then was in a state of near collapse) seized Beijing; the Chinese general in command unwisely invited a Manchu army to help evict the rebels. The Manchus did so, and then saw no reason to leave. The last Ming emperor hanged himself, and his dynasty came to an end. Nurhachi's son proclaimed the founding of the Qing Dynasty.

The Manchus by then controlled Inner Mongolia, but that control was not secure. The Oirat confederation took the lead in trying to evict the Manchus, and under such leaders as Galdan Boshogt they swept eastward from Xinjiang into eastern Mongolia. The Oirats were neither sufficiently united nor sufficiently powerful to consolidate their gains, however, and Manchu rule endured. Moreover, the Manchus cleverly exploited the old rivalry between the Oirats and the Khalkas. Playing Inner and Outer Mongolia against each other, the Manchus in 1691 guaranteed to the Khalka leaders that their tribal rights would be respected forever. Thus winning the Khalkas to their side, the Manchus were able to crush and nearly wipe out the Oirats. Inner Mongolia was placed under direct Manchu control, ruled by Chinese bureaucrats protected by Manchu garrisons. In Outer Mongolia, the Manchus of course had no intention of honoring their promises to the Khalkas. The Manchus insisted that the Living Buddha of Urga would always have to be "discovered" in Tibet, thus severing the link between the Khalka khans and the high clergy of Lamaism. Outer Mongolia, though not divided into provinces under Chinese bureaucratic rule, was placed firmly within the Manchu Qing Dynasty's empire. Beginning in the late seventeenth century, the Manchus forced the relocation of many Mongols to prevent them from forming anti-Manchu confederations; whole tribes were moved from place to place like pieces on a chessboard. It was then that some of the western Oirats migrated all the way to the Caucasus, settling west of the Volga, where they became known as

A train of camel carts in the Gobi, early twentieth century. Mongolia on the eve of its modern national independence was isolated, poor, technologically backward, and largely forgotten by the world. Arthaud and Hébert-Stevens, *Mongolie*

Kalmuks. A Khalka revolt of 1759 was put down with great bloodshed; that marked the end of serious Mongol resistance to Manchu rule.

Defeated and demoralized, Mongolia settled into a long period of stagnation. The population, greatly reduced by the slaughters that followed their defeats by the Manchus, continued to decline, in part because as many as 40 percent of the adult males pursued monastic careers, taking vows of celibacy. Chinese merchants migrated to both Inner and Outer Mongolia under Manchu protection and soon monopolized all commerce there, controlling everything from the shops of Urga to the caravans of long-distance trade.

Russian influence also began to make itself felt in Mongolia under the Manchus. The Treaties of Nerchinsk (1689) and Kyakhta (1727), between the Russian Czars and the Qing Emperors, confirmed Manchu control in Outer Mongolia, but placed the Buriat Mongols of the Lake Baikal region within the Russian empire. During the eighteenth century a substantial caravan trade across Mongolia developed between Russia and China. Furs from Siberia passed through the Chinese-dominated commercial city of Urga on their way to Beijing, where they were traded for Chinese tea, silk, porcelain, and dried rhubarb (for medicinal purposes—it is a powerful laxative). As the Qing Dynasty began to wane following the Opium Wars, a Sino-Russian treaty of 1860 allowed Russian merchants direct access to Mongolia. Russian influence in Mongolia slowly grew thereafter; when the Qing Dynasty finally was overthrown by China's Nationalist Revolution of 1911, Mongolian patriots naturally looked to Russia for aid in rescuing Mongolia from continued Chinese control. Mongolia was about to end its long period of national decline and stagnation.

Mongolia Enters the Twentieth Century

The Mongolian Revolution

During the Russo-Japanese War of 1904–1905, Mongolia found itself caught up for the first time in modern Great Power politics. Mongolian mercenary troops were recruited by both sides and gained some exposure to modern warfare; what is more important, by a secret clause in the treaty that ended the war, Russia recognized eastern Inner Mongolia as within the Japanese sphere of influence. A few years before, Russia had signed a similar agreement with Great Britain recognizing Tibet as within the British sphere. The world of the Mongols was being divided up, and no one in Mongolia even realized it.

The first stirrings of Mongolian nationalism were felt primarily outside Outer Mongolia itself, among Russian-educated Buriats in the Lake Baikal area, and among Chinese-educated Oirats and Chakhars in Inner Mongolia. Nevertheless, a spirit of discontent, not yet organized enough to be called nationalism, was also beginning to take shape in Outer Mongolia, where Chinese economic and political domination, and the threat of Japanese encroachment, were deeply resented. In 1911, when the Republic of China was established by the revolution that overthrew the Qing Dynasty, the Living Buddha of Urga seized the opportunity to declare Mongolia's independence. (He was in effect both the secular ruler and the spiritual leader of Mongolia; his titles were Bogdo Gegen, "Prince Bogdo," and Jebtsundamba Khutukhtu, "Living Buddha.") This declaration was followed by three-way negotiations—among Russia, the Republic of China, and the Mongolian leadership under the Living Buddha of Urga—by which China and Russia recognized Mongolia's autonomy, but not independence. That is, Mongolia would be allowed to control its own internal affairs, but not its army or its foreign policy.

Discussions between representatives of Outer Mongolia and Inner Mongolia for unification of the two regions came to nothing. This was in part because of traditional tribal rivalries among Khalkas, Chakhars, and Oirats, and also in part because, as in the days of Möngke, the Outer Mongolian leadership mistrusted the Inner Mongolians as having become "too Chinese." It is unlikely that the Chinese would have permitted such a union in any case; no Chinese government would have tolerated a unified Mongolian state, whether "independent" or "autonomous," so close to the Great Wall. Moreover, even by 1911, Mongols were a minority population within Inner Mongolia, as a result of Chinese migration into that region during the nineteenth century. Many Inner Mongolian nationalist leaders soon fled to Outer Mongolia to escape Chinese control. Some Mongols also dreamed of incorporating the Buriat lands of Russia into a greater Mongolian state, but that idea had even less chance of success, because the Russians, who were Mongolia's only significant ally, would not consider it. Thousands of Buriats fled to Outer Mongolia in the next few years.

The next significant development came as a result of the Russian Revolution in 1917, which brought the Bolshevik faction of the Russian Communist Party to power. The new Soviet Russian government ("red," from the color of its revolutionary flag, as opposed to the "white" aristocratic supporters of the Czar), under the leadership of Vladimir I. Lenin, was dedicated to establishing a socialist government and society at home, and to supporting socialist revolutionary movements in all countries of the world. Japan opposed the new government (and later sent troops to Siberia to support antirevolutionary Russian forces there); in 1919, a Japanese-influenced faction in the Chinese government mounted an invasion of Outer Mongolia and forced its leaders to sign a "request" to be taken over by the government of China. Japan's aim was to protect its own economic, political, and military interests in North China by keeping the Russian Revolution from influencing Mongolia.

Mongolia soon was invaded by Russians anyway, but not by revolutionaries. A White Russian army under Baron von Ungern-Sternberg attacked Urga in October 1920, and by February 1921 had defeated the Chinese garrison there (which was abandoned by its Japanese supporters). Baron von Ungern-Sternberg then recognized the Living Buddha of Urga as the ruler of an independent Mongolia, with himself as "chief military advisor." In the next six months his troops killed as many as eighty thousand Mongols (including any who showed signs of sympathizing with the Russian Revolution), brutally repressing all Mongolian opposition. During this period of terror, two small Mongolian revolutionary groups began to play an active role in fighting against von Ungern-Sternberg's occupation: a nationalist military force under Sükhe-Baatar, an ex-soldier in the Living Buddha's armed forces, and a pro-Bolshevik group under Khorloin Choibalsan, who had been educated in Siberia. These revolutionary groups joined forces and sought help from the new Bolshevik government of the U.S.S.R. Soviet Russian forces occupied Urga in July 1921; von Ungern-Sternberg was executed two months later. In November 1921 a Mongolian-Soviet treaty was signed, recognizing Mongolia's independence.

Independent Mongolia

The Living Buddha of Urga was continued in office by Sükhe-Baatar's revolutionary force as the head of the new Mongolian state, ruling as a constitutional monarch. Actual control, though, was exercised by Sükhe-Baatar, Choibalsan, and their associates, with considerable Soviet support. Sükhe-Baatar died in 1923, and the Living Buddha died in 1924. On orders from the new government, no reincarnation of the Living Buddha was discovered, and the office was allowed to pass out of existence. The capital was renamed Ulan Bator (Ulaanbaatar), "Red Hero." With the problem of constitutional monarchy conveniently solved, the ruling party was reorganized as the Mongolian People's Revolutionary Party (M.P.R.P.). The legislature, the People's Great Khural, met for the first time, and in November 1924 declared the establishment of the Mongolian People's Republic. The new government issued postage stamps and currency, and in various other ways began to demonstrate its legitimacy as a sovereign state. Soviet troops withdrew from Mongolia in 1925.

Curiously, the Soviet Union in 1924 had also signed a treaty with the Republic of China, recognizing Chinese sovereignty over Outer Mongolia and referring to the territory as an "integral part of the Republic of China." This apparent betrayal of Soviet support for an independent Mongolia in fact had very little to do with Mongolia at all, and it is clear that the Soviets had no intention of honoring that treaty. It was rather part of a political game designed to increase Soviet influence in China.

Lenin died in 1924, and China's great Nationalist hero Sun Yat-sen died in 1925. The passing from the scene of the first generation of revolutionary leaders in Mongolia's two huge neighbors brought Stalin to power in the U.S.S.R. and Chiang Kai-shek to power in China. Choibalsan, the sole surviving leader of the Mongolian revolution, seemingly was left in a dominant position within the Mongolian People's Revolutionary Party, but he was by no means master of his own fate. For the next decade, various party factions contended for power with no single leader dominant for long; party leadership reflected primarily the shifting winds of policy in Stalin's Russia.

Choibalsan's position as leader was finally strengthened by external events. The increasing threat of Japanese military activity on the Mon-

Sükhe-Baatar and Revolutionary Nationalism

Sükhe-Baatar, one of the fathers of the Mongolian People's Republic, seems to have been in real life a genuinely heroic and admirable person. Since his death he has been elevated to the stature of a national hero and a symbol of revolutionary nationalism, embodying all of the characteristics that the ruling party hopes will serve as an inspiration to the Mongolian people. In this passage from S. Nachukdorji's "Life of Sukebatur," traditional literary elements are skillfully blended with modern Marxist terminology to paint a picture of a larger-than-life figure. Sükhe-Baatar has just departed for a battle against Chinese-supported counter-revolutionary forces, as leader of a machine-gun battalion:

When Comrade Sukebatur left on this campaign his father-in-law had offered him a bowl of milk, saying, to speed him on his way with blessing:

> *Go and crush the enemy*
> *Go and come back with the title of Darkhan [hero];*
> *Go and defeat the foe*
> *Go and come back with glory and fame.*

And in fact Sukebatur did return from the battle of Khalkha River with the honorary title of Darkhan.

Thus Sukebatur, repeatedly going on active service for Mongolia, showed by his actions how devoted he was to Motherland and people, by heroically fighting like this without thought for his life and person, like a true patriot. Not only was Comrade Sukebatur a hero himself, but he was one who could inspire heroism in others. At the battle of the Khalkha River a soldier named Setergei Tashi who was under Sukebatur's command was lacking in courage and afraid of combat, and just crouched down hiding himself behind a rock. Sukebatur saw this and said harshly, "Are you going to fight Babojab? Or are you going to die at my hand? Is this the way for a man and a soldier to behave? Let's go where the bullets are falling!" Because of this, Tashi from then on gave up his being afraid and hiding and became a very fine combat soldier, and Sukebatur used to praise him highly. Tashi repeatedly used to say, "Sukebatur made a brave man of me." Thus Sukebatur inspired with heroism not just one Tashi, but many and many a Tashi.

From S. Nachukdorji, "Life of Sukebatur," translated by Owen Lattimore and Urgunge Onon, in Lattimore, *Nationalism and Revolution in Mongolia* (New York: Oxford University Press, 1955), pp. 115–16.

golian border in the 1930's (including a Japanese invasion of Manchuria in 1931) led to a ten-year treaty of friendship and mutual defense between Mongolia and the Soviet Union in 1935. By the following year, needing stability within Mongolia, Stalin gave his decisive backing to Choibalsan as the leader of the Mongolian People's Revolutionary Party. The Japanese threat to Mongolia continued to increase with the outbreak of full-scale war between Japan and China in 1937, and was forestalled only with the victory of a combined Soviet-Mongolian army over an invading Japanese force in the Battle of Nomonhan in 1939.

For nearly three years, during 1936–1939, a series of purges within the M.P.R.P. resulted in the arrest, and sometimes the execution, of Choibalsan's rivals. At the same time, a nationwide campaign against "feudal" institutions brought about the destruction of many Buddhist

The caravan of the American Museum of Natural History's Central Asian Expedition, 1925. At the time of the Mongolian Revolution, Mongolia had virtually no paved roads; all goods moved by caravan. Neg. no. 410960 (Photo by Shackelford), Courtesy Department of Library Services, American Museum of Natural History

monasteries, the confiscation of monastic property, and the forcible
return to lay life of tens of thousands of monks. Until that time socialism
had had relatively little impact on the country except among the politically active intellectual elite and a comparatively small number of urban
workers. A few steps had been taken toward modernization—railroad
construction, the establishment of radio and telegraph communications,
and some industrial development—but the countryside felt little
change. With Choibalsan securely established as the country's leader,
however, the serious transformation of Mongolia into a socialist state
began.

In the summer of 1939 fierce fighting broke out between Japanese
and Soviet-Mongolian forces near the Khalkhyn River on the border
between Mongolia and Manchuria. But this died down after several

*This village of yurts is a suburb of Ulan Bator. Note the electric power lines, and the small
factories in the left background where many of the village people probably work.* Arthaud
and Hébert-Stevens, *Mongolie*

months, and the Soviet Union did not declare war on Japan until 1945. The Soviets played no role in the Pacific campaigns of World War II, but Red Army troops and advisors were a very conspicuous presence in Mongolia throughout the war. In the spring of 1940 the tenth party congress of the M.P.R.P. confirmed Choibalsan as party leader, and adopted a new constitution that provided for a more rapid and decisive socialist transformation of the country.

As World War II drew to a close, a treaty of friendship and cooperation was signed on August 14, 1945, between the U.S.S.R. and the Republic of China, under which China recognized the independence of Mongolia provided that independence would be confirmed by a vote of the Mongolian people. In October 1945 the Mongols voted by a reported total of 430,000 to zero for independence. The following year, Mongolia and the Soviet Union signed another ten-year renewable treaty of friendship and mutual defense.

The Mongolian People's Republic

The basic structure of government was established in the early days of the republic, and the boundaries of provinces *(aimags)* and counties were laid out. The political system was closely modeled on that of the U.S.S.R. The ruling party—the only party—decided all questions of policy; legislation was ratified by the People's Great Khural, which was chosen every three (now four) years in elections in which essentially no opposition was permitted. In the postwar period, building on that basic structure, the M.P.R. began to assume the form that it has retained to the present day.

In 1946 the Cyrillic alphabet was adopted as the official means of writing the Mongolian language. This effectively cut off subsequent generations of Mongols from their own written history. The establish-

ment of a National University provided for the training of a new generation of intellectuals literate in the new written language and thoroughly
versed in Marxism and Soviet revolutionary history. A State Public
Library was founded, housing a vast collection of Buddhist scriptures
and other manuscripts in Mongolian, Tibetan, and Chinese, preserving
them for posterity but also removing them from their former place as
part of the religious life of the nation. A number of national museums
were created in former palaces and Lamaist temples; they also both
preserve and isolate religious art. Again following the Soviet model, a
National Academy of Sciences was established to place scientific research under central control, and to make leading intellectuals direct
employees of the state. "Mass organizations," such as trade unions, the
Mongolian Women's Committee, the Young Pioneers, and the Mongolian Young Revolutionary League, were established to replace traditional centers of group activity, such as clans and temples, and to give
people a sense of direct participation in the revolutionary process.

In 1948 the First Five-Year Plan was announced for the development
of the Mongolian economy. Successive five-year plans have been followed ever since. The use of five-year plans, another direct imitation
of Soviet practice, places the entire Mongolian economy under the
control of the central government; targets are set for development in
various sectors of the economy, and a national system of planning and
management is responsible for meeting those targets. With massive
Soviet assistance, the building of the foundations of an industrial economy was greatly accelerated; railroads and roads were extended and
improved, more mines were opened, electric power generating stations
were built, and apartment houses and dormitories began to replace yurts
in Ulan Bator and other industrializing cities. China also sent battalions
of workers to Mongolia, which was chronically short of labor, to aid in
industrial development.

The Chinese civil war that had broken out into the open between Nationalist and Communist forces after World War II ended in 1949 with the establishment of the People's Republic of China. The P.R.C. immediately established diplomatic relations with the M.P.R., and soon the two countries signed treaties defining their common boundary and guaranteeing friendship and cooperation. China was in no position, in the early 1950's, to provide significant financial assistance to Mongolia, being itself a major recipient of Soviet aid at that time; but the presence of a friendly socialist state on Mongolia's southern border was reassuring to the M.P.R. as it began its own process of socialist transformation. The government of the Republic of China, in exile on Taiwan, in 1953 repudiated its 1945 recognition of the M.P.R., but that action had only symbolic significance.

Combines harvesting grain on a state farm. Grain production has been a key element in the economic modernization of Mongolia under the People's Republic. Arthaud and Hébert-Stevens, *Mongolie*

Choibalsan died in January 1952, and was succeeded as party leader and premier by Yumjaagiyn Tsedenbal. Tsedenbal initially made no significant changes in Choibalsan's policies. In 1958, however, he took the socialist revolution in Mongolia a large step beyond what Choibalsan had been able to accomplish. With the announcement of the Third Five-Year Plan in that year, serious efforts began to collectivize livestock herding and to introduce modern agriculture. Ownership of livestock was transferred from individual families to herding cooperatives; individuals were made shareholders of their cooperatives, and were paid according to the performance of their unit as a whole. The boundaries of cooperative pasturelands were drawn so as to be identical with the boundaries of counties, so that the cooperatives assumed administrative as well as economic functions. Large-scale state farms and cooperative farms were established to grow wheat, potatoes, fodder, and other crops; these have been continually extended in all areas of the country that are suitable for agriculture, so that Mongolia is now self-sufficient in basic foodstuffs.

The transformation of the Mongolian countryside from tribal nomadism to collective livestock herding and large-scale agriculture must have created disruption and caused some resentment. It is difficult to say, however, how strong popular resistance to these measures was. The path to socialism on the steppes was made somewhat smoother by the long period that had elapsed between the founding of the Mongolian People's Republic and the creation of new political and economic structures in the countryside. People knew that changes were coming, and had time to get used to the idea. Memories of the squalor and poverty of prerevolutionary times were still very much alive in the 1950's as well; people thought of the bad old days, and were willing to give a new system the benefit of the doubt.

By the end of the 1950's, the Mongolian People's Republic had assumed essentially its modern form. Mongolia's transformation from a demoralized and poverty-stricken backwater to a modernizing socialist state did not come about without significant costs to the Mongolian people. Economic modernization meant the abolition of most private property, the adoption of a clumsy and inefficient mechanism of central planning, and considerable environmental damage. Freedom from China was gained at the cost of subservience to the Soviet Union; in the 1960's and 1970's, Mongolia would again become a pawn in Great Power politics, as relations between formerly friendly Communist China and the Soviet Union deteriorated into open hostility. The construction of a centralized political state went hand in hand with an almost total loss of political and religious freedom, and severe restrictions on intellectual freedom.

Nevertheless, for most Mongols the price of national independence and modernization probably seemed worth paying, at least initially. As Mongolia cautiously and gradually began to shed its Soviet-dominated isolation from the 1960's onward to enter more widely into international diplomatic and trade relations, some sense of the narrowness of the Mongolian road to socialism slowly began to emerge into the consciousness of at least some Mongolian leaders. As Mongolia enters the decade of the 1990's, winds of change are beginning to be felt in both the country's domestic and international affairs.

Culture and the Arts

Mongolian art and culture have deep roots in the ancient traditions of the steppe, stretching back to the time of Genghis Khan and beyond.* Poetry, music, dance, and sports in particular represent Mongolian culture in a pure, traditional form. At the same time, many aspects of Mongolian culture, particularly in religion, scholarship, theater, and painting, reveal strong influences from contacts with other peoples encountered at the time of the Mongol Empire and in later periods.

---

*In previous chapters we have used the word "culture" (as in the phrase "steppe culture") to refer to a society's entire system of adaptations to its environment. In this chapter, "culture" is used in its more restricted sense of "the artistic, intellectual, and spiritual aspects of life."

Religion

Shamanism and Buddhism

Before the time of Genghis Khan, the Mongols believed in a kind of nature religion similar to that of many other peoples of northern Asia. Nature gods, such as *Kökö Möngke Tenggri*, the Eternal Blue Sky, were worshiped with sacrificial rituals. The sun and moon, the earth, and prominent natural features such as mountains, rivers, and lakes were all believed to be animated by their own gods. Religious leaders called shamans (or, in the case of women, *shamankas*) communicated in a state of trance with gods and ancestral spirits on behalf of the people, and acted as healers. Shamanic rituals often included the use of special magical objects, along with music and masked dances.

Under Genghis Khan and his successors, the rulers of the Mongol Empire displayed a remarkable spirit of toleration toward the religions of the areas that they conquered. Buddhism, Islam, Christianity, and other religions were given equal protection. Many Mongols converted to these faiths; Buddhism became particularly important, but Islam and an Asian form of Christianity called Nestorianism also had some impact. Berke, the grandson of Genghis Khan who ruled the Russian portion of the Mongol Empire, became a Muslim, as did many other Mongols of the Golden Horde. Kubilai Khan became a patron of Buddhism. At the same time, the beliefs and practices of shamanism retained their importance.

After the collapse of the Mongol Empire in the fourteenth century, Buddhism came to play an increasingly important role in Mongolian culture. Lamaism, a Tibetan form of Buddhism that emphasized scriptural studies and elaborate ceremonies carried out by monks within

An old monk at the Gandan Monastery, standing before a stone statue of the Buddha.

large temples, became the national religion. Because of their common religion, strong cultural ties were formed between Mongolia and Tibet. Although religious belief now plays only a small role, formally at least, in the lives of most citizens of the Mongolian People's Republic, the cultural imprint of Lamaism remains very evident.

Religion and the Arts

Religious art makes up a large part of Mongolia's heritage in painting and sculpture. Because those arts were of little importance to the nomadic laity, they flourished almost

Lamaism

Buddhism originated in northern India around 500 B.C., when Siddartha Gautama, known as the Buddha ("Enlightened One"), began to preach a new doctrine of salvation. Gautama preached that all life involves suffering, and that because of their attachment to life, people remain trapped in a cycle of endless reincarnations in the world of suffering. But the false attachment to life can be overcome through meditation and good deeds, leading to the liberation of the soul and an end to the cycle of rebirths.

Buddhism was at first an ascetic, monastic religion, but within two centuries a sect of Buddhism called Mahayana ("Greater Vehicle") taught that salvation could be had by anyone who called on the grace of Buddhist saints. With this, Buddhism became a religious mass movement and began to spread throughout Asia.

Many centuries later, Mahayana Buddhism blended with the ancient Bon religion of Tibet to form a sect known as Lamaism. The

exclusively within Lamaistic temples. Paintings called *tankas* were an essential feature of every temple's decoration. Some were brought to Mongolia from Tibet, while others were produced locally by Mongolian monks. *Tankas* portray the various gods and saints of Lamaistic Buddhism; although they were created primarily as objects of religious devotion, they are also often very beautiful. Similarly, small sculptures of gilt bronze, depicting gods and saints, were usually displayed on temple altars. Today, these paintings and sculptures are cherished as works of art rather than as objects of religious devotion. The National

old Tibetan gods and demons became symbols of a Buddhist struggle between good and evil. Lamaism became a monastic religion, centered in great temples; in Tibet, and later in Mongolia, most families encouraged at least one son to become a monk in order to win religious merit for the entire family. Monasteries are headed by chief monks called lamas; each lama is thought to be a physical reincarnation of his predecessor. Various branches of Lamaism are headed by grand lamas, of whom the greatest is the Dalai Lama, the spiritual head of all Tibetan and Mongolian Buddhists.

Lamaism maintains the basic original doctrines of Mahayana Buddhism, but has evolved its own forms of religious practice. The soul's struggle against evil is made visible in religious paintings and statues of gods like the serene Tara, and of demons like Yama the Destroyer. A wide variety of sacred objects, such as drums and trumpets made from the skulls and thigh bones of famous lamas, are thought to have magic powers in driving away the demons that symbolize the world's evil powers.

Museum of Fine Arts in Ulan Bator contains an outstanding collection of Lamaistic paintings, sculpture, and other religious objects. In the twentieth century modern oil painting, sculpture, and other secular fine arts have begun to play a role in Mongolia's artistic life.

Because most Mongols lived in yurts until very recently, Mongolia developed no native tradition of permanent architecture. Except for a few brick or adobe commercial buildings in the market towns, architecture as such was confined to the creation of temples and palaces. Temples, always built in Tibetan style, were massive structures of stone, often faced with stucco, rising several stories high and topped with Chinese-style tile roofs. Palaces, even those built within the grounds of a temple, were always built in pure Chinese style, with wooden post-and-beam construction and massive tile roofs supported by elaborate wooden brackets. The outstanding surviving example of palace architecture is the Bogdo Genen Palace in Ulan Bator, the former winter palace of the Grand Lama of Mongolia, now a museum.

Lamaistic temples were communities of monks (and sometimes also of nuns), whose function was to pray and carry out religious ceremonies on behalf of all the people of the country. They also often possessed extensive libraries of books in Tibetan, Mongolian, Chinese, and Sanskrit (the language of ancient India), and theological studies formed part of the training of every monk. Temples took the place of universities in traditional Mongolian society, and individual monks might study not only theology, but also such subjects as astronomy and astrology, mathematics, and medicine.

Temples served as centers of community life, places where scattered groups of nomads might gather on special occasions. Religious holidays

Religious painting (tanka) of Green Tara, one of the principal deities of Lamaistic Buddhism. Mongolian religious art is typically done in pure Tibetan style, reflecting the origins of Mongolian Lamaistic Buddhism.

were festive occasions, with worship services that included processions, music, and the chanting of scriptures. Monks wearing masks and elaborate costumes performed ritual dances to exorcise evil spirits. Such holidays often provided the occasion for public festivals called *naadam* that might include livestock fairs, performances of music and plays, and sports competitions. In this way, religious centers provided a focus for Mongolian secular culture.

Buddha and Marx

Religion often helps people to understand themselves and to form bonds with other believers. Religion, or some other system of beliefs that plays a role equivalent to that of religion in society, seems to be an essential element of almost every national culture of the world. This was certainly true in Mongolia before modern

The Bogdo Genen Palace, Ulan Bator. This palace, formerly the winter residence of the Living Buddha of Urga—ruler of both church and state in prerevolutionary Mongolia, and sometimes known as the "God-King"—is built in Chinese style, with post-and-beam construction and a heavy tile roof. The palaces of the thirteenth-century Great Khans of the Mongol Empire at Karakorum were also built in this style, although they were larger and more elaborate.

times: Buddhism was the national religion of Mongolia, and it played an important part in the lives of the Mongolian people. Today, however, formal religion is only a minor factor in Mongolian national life.

With the coming of the Communist revolution to the Soviet Union and Mongolia around 1920, and to China in 1949, the role of religion among the Mongol populations of all three countries was drastically restricted. Marxist revolutionary leaders criticized the traditional Lamaist temples as centers of wealth and idleness, a burden on the economic life of the people and a distraction from the essential work of modernization.

In Mongolia and the Mongol regions of the Soviet Union, temples were dismantled or abandoned, their scriptures and religious images were scattered or destroyed, and monks were returned to the ordinary work force. Not surprisingly, this suppression of religion was widely resented, but at the same time the government's actions could be explained and justified to the people, at least to some extent, because many temples had become corrupt, decadent, and excessively wealthy at the people's expense. Except for a few temples kept alive as showcases of traditional culture, Buddhism as an organized religion was nearly wiped out. In China, where the revolution occurred a generation later and where the revolutionary government took a somewhat tolerant attitude toward the religions of minority peoples, Buddhism came under less severe pressure, and many Mongols in China's Inner Mongolian Autonomous Region and Xinjiang Province continue to practice Lamaistic Buddhism and maintain close religious and cultural ties to Tibet.

Nevertheless, most Mongols today live in Socialist countries—Mongolia, the Soviet Union, and China—where the governments are officially atheistic and hostile to religion. Most young people receive no formal religious training, and after several generations under Communist rule, religious practices in the home are fading away. Karl Marx has replaced Buddha; a secular, "scientific" social order rather than religious salvation is the official basis of Mongolian education and national values today. Nevertheless, despite this radical ideological transformation, Mongolian national culture today contains strong traditional elements as well as a vigorous spirit of modernism.

The Arts

Music and Dance   Music and dance are among the most characteristic elements of Mongolian culture, and indeed the Mongols are one of the world's most musical peoples. Music, and especially vocal music, penetrates almost every aspect of Mongolian life.

Mongolian musical instruments comprise only a few basic types, and most instrumental music is played as an accompaniment to singing. The most typical Mongolian musical instrument, regarded as basic to any performance, is the *morin khuur*, or horse-head fiddle. The horse-head fiddle is often played in ensemble with the *tovshuur* and the *shudraga*, two kinds of banjolike stringed instruments. These very ancient instruments apparently originated in steppe culture, and have now spread all across Asia; similar instruments are found everywhere from Iran to Japan. Other instruments include both transverse and vertical flutes, drums, and a variety of cymbals, gongs, and tambourines.

Mongolian vocal music, which is inseparable from Mongolian poetry, includes several different styles and genres.

Folk songs embrace a variety of themes, but herding songs and work songs are the most prominent. Mongolian herders constantly sing to their animals; there are a great many traditional melodies with very specific uses in controlling animals. For example, there are songs to call animals that have strayed away from the herd or flock, songs to comfort ewes during the lambing season, even a special song to coax a ewe into

The Morin Khuur

The *morin khuur*, or horse-head
fiddle, is to Mongolian music
what the guitar is to American
folk music—the indispensable
instrument. It takes its name
from the horse head that is
always carved at the end of the
fingerboard, above the tuning
pegs. The body of the
instrument is trapezoidal, and
is covered with a leather
sounding board. It has two
strings, usually tuned to an
interval of a fifth. As its name
implies, the horse-head fiddle
is played with a bow, which is
made of wood and horsehair.
The *morin khuur* is played with
the musician seated, resting the
instrument on his knee.
Traditionally, in many parts of
Mongolia, every adult male was
expected to be able to play the
morin khuur; to be unable to do
so was to be less than a man.

adopting and nursing an orphan lamb. Work songs are sung during tasks done by groups of people, such as taking down or setting up camp during the migration seasons. Herding songs and work songs are sometimes sung with an instrumental accompaniment, but they more frequently are unaccompanied. Also included in the folk song category are songs in praise of famous horses; these often are sung accompanied by the *morin khuur* and other instruments, and feature a cadence that imitates the gait of a horse.

Yurol are songs of ritual blessing for special occasions; they are, essentially, chanted or sung versions of traditional poetic blessings. All important events, such as the opening of a wrestling match, archery contest, or horse race, or setting out on a long journey, are begun with the singing of a blessing.

Related to songs of blessing are *maagtal*, or songs of praise. These are usually performed by groups of singers and instrumentalists, and are an important part of any festive occasion. Praise songs are lively, robust, and very melodic; they usually are sung in praise of features of the Mongolian landscape that traditionally have been considered especially beautiful or even sacred. Popular *maagtal*, known throughout Mongolia, include the "Praise Song to the Altai Mountains," the "Praise Song to the Kerulen River," and many others.

Some kinds of Mongolian songs are usually performed by professional singers rather than by ordinary people. *Khurchins*, professional ballad singers (almost always men), were often employed in the past to entertain at festivals by singing epic songs about legendary and historical heroes and their deeds of bravery; accompanying himself on the

An outdoor musical performance at the Bogdo Genen Palace, Ulan Bator. The singer, in traditional dress, is performing an urtyn duu *("long song"); the musicians play the transverse flute and the* morin khuur *(horse-head fiddle).* Photo courtesy of the Mongolian State Folk Song and Dance Ensemble

morin khuur or the *tovshuur*, the ballad singer would perform for hours on end. *Urtyn duu*, or "long songs," are musical settings of lyrical poetry; these too are sung by professional singers using a difficult and intricate operatic style that requires many years of training.

Mongolian vocal music includes not only singing as such, but also a variety of other vocal sounds, such as tongue clicks, humming, and whistling. The most remarkable music of this sort is *khoomei*, or "harmonic singing." The *khoomei* singer (almost always a man, because of the great strength of abdominal and throat muscles required) uses his chest and diaphragm to set up a constant, bagpipelike bass note, and then simultaneously uses his throat and nasal passages to create high harmonic notes and melodic whistling. The effect of the one-man performance sounds like two or three people singing together. The origins of this kind of harmonic singing are obscure. Mongolian scholars insist that it originated in Mongolian folk music, but a similar technique is employed by Tibetan monks for some temple rituals. It is possible, therefore, that *khoomei* singing came to Mongolia along with Lamaism; it is also possible that the influence flowed in the other direction.

The richness and variety of Mongolian music are very striking. Although Mongolian music is still very little known in the West, visitors to Mongolia are almost invariably impressed by the beauty of the country's music, and by the extent to which it enriches the lives of the people of the steppe.

Some Mongolian music, particularly instrumental music, is intended specifically to accompany dancing. Mongolian dance includes a number of kinds of group folk dance similar to round dancing and square dancing; these might be performed by groups of men, groups of women, or groups of mixed couples. These dances are normally performed outdoors, as are the dances called *bujig*, performed by men and featuring vigorous leg movements similar to the dances of the Russian Cossacks. The most typical Mongolian dance form, however, is the *bii* or *biyelge*, "upper-body dance." A *biyelge* is normally performed by women, and was intended to be performed within the confined space of a yurt. Accordingly, leg movements are restricted or entirely absent; some forms of *biyelge* are performed in a sitting or kneeling position. The dance consists of intricate, rhythmic movements of the head, shoulders, arms, and upper torso; some dancers display their skill by dancing with bowls of tea or *airag* balanced on their wrists, elbows, and heads.

Traditional music and dance continue to flourish in Mongolia today, and are encouraged by the Mongolian State Folk Song and Dance Ensemble. Modern Western music and dance have also entered contemporary Mongolian national life; the State Orchestra, State Opera, and State Ballet perform a wide range of works from the classical Western repertory. Soviet-style rock music has also made its appearance in the night life of Ulan Bator.

Literature

Apart from religious scriptures, much of Mongolia's traditional literature existed, until recently, primarily as oral literature: poetry designed to be recited, chanted, or sung; stories told around campfires and at festivals and marketplaces. In modern times Mongolian scholars have collected much of this oral literature and preserved it in written form.

Poetry was part of the daily life of every Mongol in traditional times, and remains so to some extent today. Poems formed the texts of Mongolia's rich heritage of songs, and also were incorporated into everyday conversation in the form of poetic blessings. For example, someone seeing a woman weaving or doing embroidery might say a traditional rhymed blessing: "May thy hand be skillful and the work a success." Such blessings were spoken on many occasions; there is a blessing for sending a letter, another for receiving one, a blessing for setting out on a journey and a blessing for welcoming guests, and so on.

Riddles and jokes, of which Mongols are extremely fond, also fall into the category of conversational poetry. Poetry also was found in the form of "cross-talk," a witty and prolonged exchange of rhymed remarks. Skill in such conversation was an admired social grace. Rhyming was even formalized as a substitute for fighting. The "poetry fight" was a public exchange of rhymed insults between enemies (usually men); the first one to lose his temper was declared the loser of the battle. At that point, honor demanded that the quarrel should be forgotten. (Contemporary American rap music originated, in part, from a similar feature of African-American urban culture—"the dozens," an exchange of witty insults.)

Much of the epic poetry of Mongolia was preserved in the memories of professional bards, but some was written down at an early date. The outstanding example of a written epic is *The Secret History of the Mongols*, a long poem telling of the rise to power of Genghis Khan and the formation of his empire. It was written down in the mid-to-late thirteenth century, and, as its name suggests, it was not supposed to be revealed to non-Mongols.

Folktales were also a part of Mongolian oral literature; many traditional tales have now been collected and written down. Folktales embraced many themes, from love stories and heroic deeds to stories of the supernatural. A favorite type was the humorous tale, often featuring the exploits of Dalan Khuldalchi, a Paul Bunyan-like folk hero, or else the wily tricks of the *baldarchins*, wandering monks who lived by their wits.

Theater is not a prominent feature in the lives of nomadic people, but a Mongolian theatrical tradition did exist in market towns and in temples. During the Mongol Yuan Dynasty in China (1270–1368), the Mongol rulers became extremely fond of Chinese opera, and Chinese-style opera troupes began to perform in Mongolia as well. Traditional

Mongolian theater quickly developed its own scripts in Mongolian, featuring plots with Mongolian themes, but stylistically its roots in Chinese theater remained clear. Lamaistic temples also sometimes presented theatrical performances on religious themes, to instruct as well as entertain people at temple festivals. In the late nineteenth century modern Western-style theater was introduced into Mongolia, but it reached only a small elite audience.

The circus is another popular theatrical form in Mongolia. The Mongolian circus of today has its origins in part in the traditional marketplace entertainments of jugglers and acrobats, but has been influenced by the excellent circuses of Russia. In addition to aerialists, animal acts, and clowns, the Mongolian circus makes a special feature of contortionists, gymnastic performers who can twist their arms, legs, and bodies into human pretzels.

Modern literature in Mongolia has been extensively influenced by Western, and particularly Russian, literature. Poetry remains of great importance, but new forms such as novels and short stories have also entered Mongolia's national literature. The modern era in Mongolian literature began in the early postrevolutionary period of the 1920's and 1930's, with the work of Dashdorjyn Natsagdorj and other writers. Natsagdorj's poem "My Homeland" is regarded as one of the founding works of modern Mongolian literature. Tsendyn Damdinsuren became known as the father of the modern Mongolian novel with the publication in 1929 of his greatest work, *Rejected Maiden.* Many other contemporary writers emerged in subsequent years, though their work suffers to some extent from the requirement that it stick to socialist themes. For example, in the 1930's Damdinsuren himself wrote short stories and film scripts that attempted to create a new type of Mongolian hero, the socialist revolutionary worker. In contrast, the best-known modern Mongolian writer, Y. Rinchen, has largely rejected Soviet literary mod-

els, and sees his own work as rooted in Mongolian nationalism. His three-volume historical novel about the Mongolian revolution, *Rays of Dawn*, was written during the 1950's.

The Mongolian literary scene today is active and lively. The magazine *Tsog (The Spark)* publishes the work of many contemporary writers. The State Drama Theater, founded in 1931, performs both Western and modern Mongolian works, while the Mongolkino studio produces films from the scripts of Mongolian screenwriters. Contemporary Mongolian films range from rather dreary "boy meets tractor" socialist dramas to finely produced historical epics like *Proud Eagle*, the story of a champion wrestler in prerevolutionary times.

Sports and Games

The "three manly games," horse racing, archery, and wrestling, have been central to Mongolian cultural life for centuries. They continue to be practiced with great enthusiasm today, and form the highlights of the great National Naadam festival held in each province and county of Mongolia on July 11 of every year, the anniversary day of the 1921 Mongolian Revolution. Winners of local club contests compete at these meets for titles and places on a national ranking system; national champions win admiration and fame.

Mongolian horseracing is similar to Western steeplechase racing, because the races are conducted overland rather than on closed-circuit tracks. Races are held for riders of all ages, but at the National Naadam,

A Mongol archer demonstrating the technique of shooting birds overhead with a compound bow. The powerful compound bow has remained essentially unchanged in design for over two thousand years. Skill in its use was taken for granted among all adult Mongols, at least until very recent times. Arthaud and Hébert-Stevens, *Mongolie*

the featured race is in the children's division. Children from seven to twelve years of age, dressed in traditional costumes, race over a 20-mile cross-country course, displaying a skill in horsemanship possible only in a country where many people learn to ride in infancy.

Archery contests feature the ancient Mongolian compound bow, short but powerful enough to propel a heavy arrow for several hundred yards. Contestants, in both men's and women's divisions, compete both from horseback and from a standing position, aiming at a leather target of traditional design. Champions are awarded such poetic titles as Supermarksman and Miraculous Archer.

Mongolian wrestling is the most distinctive of the three manly games. Contestants wear a colorful traditional costume consisting of tight-fitting briefs; a tight vest that covers the back, shoulders, and upper arms, but leaves the chest bare; and heavy leather boots. The distinctive wrestling vest is said to be a way of making it obvious that neither of the contestants is a woman. Legend has it that hundreds of years ago a champion wrestler was discovered to be a woman in disguise, which greatly embarrassed the many men she had defeated.

The wrestlers enter the ring with slow, exaggerated steps, arms extended at their sides, dipping and swooping in imitation of the magical Garuda bird of Buddhist legend. When the referee starts a match, the wrestlers grab each others' vests, and each tries, with a variety of throws, tripping kicks, and other maneuvers, to topple the other. The first wrestler to touch the ground with anything other than the soles of his feet loses. When the match is over, the loser kneels and the winner passes his hand over the loser's head in a sign of victory. Champion wrestlers, like archers, receive colorful titles, such as Titan, Lion, Elephant, and Falcon.

A wrestling match. The first wrestler to be knocked to the ground loses. Wrestling, one of the traditional "three manly sports," remains tremendously popular in Mongolia today.

Along with the three manly games, chess may be regarded as a Mongolian national sport. Introduced from India via Persia in ancient times, Mongolian chess has some pieces that are different from those of familiar Western chess—a camel in place of a bishop, for example— but is played according to similar rules.

Today, a wide range of modern sports is found in Mongolia; basketball and soccer enjoy great popularity. Mongolian athletes regularly participate in the Olympics, and have done particularly well in modern archery, gymnastics, weight lifting, and target shooting. Thus in sports, as in many other areas, Mongolia has succeeded in preserving a rich traditional national life while participating in the internationalized Western culture of modern times.

Daily Life

Slightly more than half the people of Mongolia now live in cities and towns. For them, daily life is not very different from that in many other developing countries of the Third World; such differences as there are relate primarily to diet, dress, customs, and other aspects of culture. In the Mongolian countryside, daily life is much closer to the traditional life of Mongols in premodern times, although even in rural areas, modernization has brought significant changes.

Rural Life

As in premodern times, life in rural Mongolia revolves around the daily needs of the huge flocks of sheep and goats, and herds of horses, cattle, or camels, tended by the people. The work is highly seasonal, with different tasks for every time of the year.

Spring is the busiest season, the time when lambs and kids are born; then, every member of every rural household spends hours in the pasturelands helping with difficult births, ensuring that ewes are able to nurse their young, and performing other essential tasks. Newborn colts, calves, and other animals must be tended to. As summer approaches, sheep must be shorn for the yearly crop of wool, while cashmere goats are combed to harvest their soft underwool.

Summer is a relatively relaxed season, a time when flocks and herds have ample pasture and need only be tended and given water as they graze. It is a time to enjoy the pleasures of life. About one out of every six Mongols belongs to some kind of amateur arts organization, such as a music group or theatrical club, and these groups make an important contribution to the cultural life of rural areas. On July 11, Mongolia's national holiday, everyone celebrates with festivals that include sports competitions and performances of music and dance. Traditional foods are sold at outdoor stands, and everyone has a chance to relax and be sociable with often far-flung neighbors.

As autumn approaches a crucial difference between premodern and contemporary Mongolia becomes evident: Mongolia is no longer primarily a nomadic society. Traditionally, at the end of summer clans and tribes would gather for the migration to winter pastures. Now, except in very remote and arid areas, this has changed. Herding cooperatives have been established in place of traditional migratory grazing areas, and the widespread raising of fodder on state farms has made it no

A camel-riding shepherd driving a flock of sheep in the Gobi. Despite extensive urbanization during the twentieth century, many Mongols still live rather traditional lives in small, widely scattered livestock-raising camps and settlements. Arthaud and Hébert-Stevens, *Mongolie*

longer necessary to move the herds and flocks any significant distance. As autumn winds dry out the pastures and cold weather approaches, members of herding cooperatives round up their livestock, confine them in pens or barns, and begin to feed them hay. Breeding—sometimes, now, by artificial insemination—is attended to for the following spring's crop of young. Equipment is repaired and supplies are double-checked as both people and animals prepare to endure the hard winter ahead.

Winter comes early in Mongolia, and lasts for a long time. Howling winds, and temperatures that stay well below freezing for weeks at a time, make life difficult and sometimes miserable. Even with animals confined in pens, herders must often struggle to keep them alive. For people, however, winter is not nearly as bad as it was in the old days, when life involved either tending herds on the open range or huddling inside a smoky yurt heated by a dung fire, trying to keep warm. Coal stoves have improved both the temperature and the atmosphere of yurts in winter now, and radio and even television help the long nights pass more quickly. In some of the most prosperous areas of the steppe, people now pack up their yurts during the winter and move into brick apartment buildings in rural villages, commuting to their livestock pens by truck or on horseback.

City Life

Urga, as Mongolia's capital was once named, used to be called the "city of yurts." Modern Ulan Bator, however, is now a large city of apartment buildings. Suburbs of yurts still ring the metropolitan area, but for most urban workers, home is an apartment in a large housing complex. Apartments are often small and very basic in their equipment—in some of the older buildings, bathrooms and even kitchens are shared by two families—but they are equipped with electricity, running water, and either central heating or individual kerosene heaters. Apartment living thus simplifies the basic tasks of housekeeping and makes it easy for people to keep warm and dry in Mongolia's harsh climate.

On the other hand, city life means that more time must be spent shopping for food and traveling to work. Rural people make *airag*, cheese, yoghurt, and other staples of the Mongolian diet from their own

Ulan Bator is a modern city with a population of about half a million people. Its low skyline is filled with government buildings and modern apartment houses.

cooperative's flocks; in the city, all those things must be trucked in for people to purchase at markets. Few apartments have refrigerators, so part of a housewife's daily routine is shopping for food. As in the Soviet Union, this often involves spending hours waiting in lines at under-stocked shops. Breakfast for an urban family might be a traditional Mongol meal of *airag*, cheese, flat bread, and buttered tea, or a more "modern" Russian-style meal of pancakes and jam with side dishes of cheese and boiled eggs or canned meat.

Ulan Bator is a very large, sprawling city, and it has a real rush hour as both husbands and wives head off for work—most families have two wage earners. Most people travel to work on buses; high officials use cars supplied by their work units, but there are few private automobiles, and bicycles are of limited usefulness because of the long, frigid winters. Children walk to school or travel by bus, and the small children left behind are taken care of by grandparents living with their families, or are placed in nurseries run by the housing projects.

Work in Ulan Bator includes the whole spectrum of urban employ-ment, from white-collar jobs in government offices to professional work at hospitals, universities, and research centers, to factory work of all sorts. Many men work in the city's railroad yards, power plants, and factories; women, too, do factory work, but tend to concentrate in light industries such as textiles and food processing. Many of Mongolia's smaller cities have sprung up around single industries; in Erdenet, for example, almost everyone works in the city's copper and molybdenum mines and ore-dressing plants, or in facilities that support those indus-tries.

City life offers far more opportunities than rural life for varied leisure activities. Ulan Bator has a wide range of museums, a large public library, and movie theaters, performance halls for concerts and plays, and a resident circus. Close ties with the Soviet Union and Eastern

The First Mongol in Space

Jugderdemidiin Gurragcha has perhaps the most unusual job of anyone in the Mongolian People's Republic: He is a cosmonaut (or, as we would say, an astronaut). In the midst of his career as a fighter pilot in the Mongolian Air Force, he was selected for cosmonaut training in a joint Soviet-Mongolian space program. In 1981, along with three Soviet cosmonauts, he blasted off in a transport rocket and docked with the Salyut-6 space station, where the crew performed scientific research and tested the effects of long periods of weightlessness.

The technology that made Cosmonaut Gurragcha's flight possible was, of course, entirely Russian, but his mission was not simply a propaganda exercise on behalf of Soviet-Mongolian friendship. Rather, it is a reminder that some Mongolian graduates of the National University, various technical schools, and military training programs now have fully reached international standards of proficiency in their respective fields.

Soviet-Mongolian cooperation in space science is conspicuous on the ground as well as in orbit. Tracking stations in Mongolia, staffed by Mongolian as well as Soviet astronomers, engineers, and technicians, are an important link in controlling the many manned and unmanned satellites in the U.S.S.R.'s active space program. And data from Soviet satellites, particularly high-resolution photographic maps, has been put to good use by other Mongolian technical workers in such fields as agriculture, pastureland conservation, mineral exploration, and water resource development.

Europe often mean that people in Mongolia's cities (if they are lucky enough to get tickets) can enjoy visiting ballet, theatrical, and musical troupes from other countries in the socialist bloc. And, as in the countryside, amateur arts organizations, sports leagues, and other groups offer ample opportunities for entertainment and recreation.

Work

Whether it is an office, a factory, a mine, or even a herding collective, the workplace plays a much larger role in the lives of Mongolian workers than it does for most people in the West. (This is true in the Soviet Union and all other socialist countries as well.) The "work unit" is the basis of every Mongol's identity within society. It often supplies housing, nurseries and schools, medical clinics, recreation facilities, and other necessities of life. Workers also belong to labor unions, but because socialist societies are by definition supposed to be "workers' states," unions do not have their familiar role of bargaining with employers for higher wages and better working conditions. Rather, their role is primarily political: Unions elect representatives to the People's Great Khural and other legislative bodies, for example.

Working hours in the countryside vary according to the season, and like all agricultural workers, Mongolian herders must keep working until their tasks are done. For urban and industrial workers, however, working hours are limited by law to eight hours per day—and in difficult or dangerous occupations such as mining, six or seven hours. Retirement usually comes when workers reach their mid-fifties—earlier in the case of heavy industry, later for office workers and officials. Retired people usually live with their married children, and help to take care of the home and the grandchildren.

Education

One of the most striking differences between countryside and city in Mongolia is in education. In rural areas, children must by law attend school for four years—barely enough to achieve a basic level of literacy and mathematical competence. In cities and towns, in contrast, children attend school for a minimum of seven years. What is more important, the opportunity for further education, at the middle school, high school, and even university levels, is much more readily available to urban students than to rural ones. Most herding collectives are not large enough or wealthy enough to support more than an elementary school, so a bright child in a remote area who wanted to continue his or her education would have to travel a long distance to school after the fourth grade, or perhaps even attend a boarding school. Some people in Mongolia are beginning to express concern that the difference in educational levels between countryside and city will create a permanent opportunity gap in Mongolian society.

Nevertheless, at the beginning of this century education was almost totally unavailable except in Buddhist monasteries, and illiteracy was considered normal. Thus Mongols today are proud of their achievement in bringing the opportunity to achieve at least basic literacy to almost every child in the country. For students who are both able and lucky, the country offers education leading even to a doctorate. The National University and several technical institutes and universities offer college and postgraduate education, and some students are sent to study abroad in universities in the Soviet Union or Eastern Europe.

Many Mongolian children between the ages of ten and fifteen belong to the Young Pioneer Organization, modeled loosely on scouting organizations in the West. The Young Pioneers is partly a recreational group, but it also encourages patriotism and good citizenship, social service,

and the development of skills in sports, outdoor activities, and the arts. At age fifteen, Young Pioneers who have demonstrated both ability and good attitudes (or whose families have good political connections) might be invited to join the Mongolian Young Revolutionary League. That organization is viewed by the national ruling party as a training ground for future party members and national leaders.

Love, Marriage, and Children

In premodern Mongolia, marriages were often arranged by the parents of the prospective bride and groom without consulting them at all. Today marriage is still a family affair, and "love matches" made by two young people without consulting their parents are quite unusual. Most young people rely on their families or their work units, labor unions, clubs, or other social organizations to help them make a good match. Still, marriage has become much more of a personal affair than it used to be, and young people expect to find love as well as suitability in their marriages.

A modern Mongolian wedding ceremony is a rather simple affair, involving most importantly a formal signing of a marriage register at the local county headquarters or city hall. After that ritual, the marriage is celebrated by a traditional family feast, with special festival foods and an ample supply of vodka. The newlyweds will wear traditional festival clothing at the wedding feast, including, for the woman, elaborate fur-trimmed robes and a formal headdress and heavy jewelry. In some cases, this clothing might be a family heirloom, carefully kept for such

A group of students on a class outing to the ruins of Erdene Dzu Monastery, near Karakorum. Mongolian education emphasizes both the glory of the Mongol past and the supposedly feudal and exploitative nature of the old regime.

occasions, but nowadays, especially in cities, it is often rented for the day from the wedding photographer.

Because Mongolia is a very thinly populated country, and the government regards it as necessary to produce more workers for the future, couples are encouraged to have large families. Contraception is nearly unknown. Special allowances for large families are paid by work units, and such services as education, health care, and day-care centers are free or available at nominal cost. Children are welcomed—the more, the better—and are raised in a warm and loving environment.

As in most tribal societies, women in premodern Mongolia played a prominent role in society, although they were also clearly subservient to men. In today's Mongolia, the equal rights of women are guaranteed by law. Reality does not always measure up to theory; as is true in most societies, women often find it difficult to advance to high positions at work and in political leadership, and they often must also work a "second shift" when they come home from work, cooking dinner, taking care of children, and doing housework. Nevertheless, women do enjoy equal legal rights, including the right to divorce. But divorce is rare in Mongolian society; although it is available on a variety of grounds, it is socially discouraged. Couples in difficulty will be advised to seek counseling and the advice of members of their work groups and other social units before taking the final step.

Food and Clothing

Mongolian food is heavily based on meat and dairy products. The daily diet of most Mongols includes cheese, yoghurt, and, above all, many

A family meal inside a yurt. The setting is traditional, but the manners are modern. Formerly the men would have been served first and the women and children would have eaten only when the men had finished. Mongolia *magazine, No. 4, 73, 1983*

bowls of the lightly fermented mare's milk called *airag* (which looks and tastes like thin yoghurt). Meat—usually mutton—is grilled or stewed with onions and other cold-weather vegetables that can be grown or gathered on the steppe. Humans also need to eat carbohydrates, of course, and the Mongolian diet includes grain in the form of porridges of millet, barley, or oats, and also steamed buns, noodles, and flat bread made of wheat flour.

Khorkhog, *a Festival Dish*

Khorkhog is characteristic of Mongolian cuisine, but because it is normally made in large quantities and takes a long time to cook, it is not served on ordinary occasions; it is usually reserved for festivals. Here is the recipe:

INGREDIENTS

Meat of one sheep, left on the bone and cut into small pieces
One large basket of onions, peeled and chopped coarsely
Salt
Red pepper pods
Other herbs and spices to taste

METHOD

Mix all ingredients. Line the bottom of a large pottery urn with stones heated red-hot in the coals of a fire. Add a 2-inch layer of the meat mixture. Add another layer of hot stones. Continue alternating layers of meat mixture and hot stones until the urn is filled. Seal urn and leave undisturbed for several hours. Scooping around stones, serve meat and onions over rice; serve cooking broth in bowls at end of meal.

In premodern times only a small amount of wheat was grown in Mongolia; the establishment of state farms to cut down on the need for imported grain has been a major policy of the government of the Mongolian People's Republic. Rice, which cannot be grown in Mongolia's dry, cool climate, must be imported and remains a luxury food for special occasions. In premodern times, vegetables in Mongolian cuisine were limited largely to onions and cabbage; early visitors to the steppe frequently complained of the boredom of a diet that included few green vegetables. This situation has improved considerably, as carrots, potatoes, and other root crops, and beans, sweet corn, and other vegetables, are increasingly grown locally. The shortage of suitable farmland and the short growing season continue to limit the supply of fresh green vegetables, however. Perhaps a more important dietary change has been the widespread availability in Mongolia of canned vegetables from the Soviet Union and Eastern Europe.

The Mongolian diet also includes many daily cups of tea, which is often served in Tibetan style, mixed with butter and roasted barley. Especially among more "modern" city dwellers, tea is sometimes served Russian style, in a tall glass and sweetened with fruit preserves, or Western style, with milk and sugar. Tea, jam, and sugar are all imported products; tea is usually readily available, but sweets are sometimes in short supply.

Mongolian clothing reflects the close relationship between people and their flocks and herds. The basic outfit for both men and women consists of trousers and a long robe—called a *deel*—that is slit at each side for ease in riding. The clothing itself is made of silk or cotton cloth (or, now, sometimes of synthetic fabrics). Heavy winter cloaks are lined and trimmed with fleece or fur. Both men and women wear high, heavy leather boots that are often richly tooled and dyed. Men and women also wear hats made of leather or felt, trimmed with fur. The shape of these hats varies among different Mongolian tribes and subtribes, providing an instantly recognizable badge of identification.

In rural areas, many people habitually wear traditional clothing, or a mixture of Mongolian and Western clothes. In cities and towns, many people now wear ordinary Western-style clothing; industrial workers typically wear work clothes of heavy blue cotton. Until very recently, in fact, the government actively discouraged urban Mongols from wearing traditional clothing, hoping thereby to promote modern (that is to say, Western) attitudes along with Western dress. Now that attitude has relaxed, and traditional clothing is often worn in the cities as well, and eagerly sought in department stores.

A Polite Society

Mongolian society places very strong emphasis on politeness and hospitality. In the nomadic society of premodern times, the population was spread very thinly across the vast steppes, and visitors were a welcome distraction from the isolation of daily life. On the other hand, visitors might sometimes be hostile, and the elaborate rituals of greetings, exchanges of poetic blessings, and the offering of hospitality served to defuse the potentially tense situations that might arise when strangers suddenly appeared in a nomad camp.

One interesting example of formal Mongolian etiquette is the snuff-bottle ritual. After the introduction of tobacco into Asia from the New

Traditional Khalka Mongol winter costumes for men and women. The outer robes are of padded silk (from China) trimmed with fur. Note also the heavy leather boots for both sexes, and the woman's elaborate headdress, consisting of a stiffened wig and heavy silver ornaments. In many nomadic societies around the world, wealth (which must be portable) is displayed in the form of women's jewelry. U. Yadamsuren, *National Costumes of the M.P.R.*, State Publishing House, Ulan Bator, 1967, plates 2 & 27

Buttered Tea

Tea served in Tibetan style, mixed with butter and roasted barley, has been a popular drink in Mongolia for centuries. The English traveler John Bell described his first encounter with this unusual beverage during his trip to Mongolia in the early eighteenth century:

The hospitable landlady immediately set her kettle on the fire. . . . She took care to wipe it very clean with a horse's tail that hung in a corner of the tent for that purpose; then the water was put into it, and soon after, some coarse bohea tea, which is got from China, and a little salt. When near boiling, she took a large brass ladle and tossed the tea, till the liquor turned very brown. It was now taken off the fire and, after subsiding a little, was poured clear into another vessel. The kettle being wiped clean with the horse's tail, as before, was again set upon the fire. The mistress now prepared a paste, of meal and fresh butter, that hung in a skin near the horse's tail, which

World in the seventeenth century, Mongols adopted the Chinese custom of using snuff—powdered tobacco intended to be inhaled, not smoked—carried in small bottles made of porcelain or carved from jade, agate, or other semiprecious stone. Both snuff and snuff bottles were important items of trade from China to Mongolia. Snuff became part of the Mongolian ritual of greetings; when two Mongols met, they would take out their snuff bottles and offer them to each other, and the act

was put into the tea-kettle and fried. Upon this paste the tea was again poured; to which was added some good thick cream, taken out of a clean sheep's skin. . . . The ladle was again employed, for the space of six minutes, when the tea, being removed from the fire, was allowed to stand a while in order to cool. . . . The principal advantage of this tea is, that it both satisfies hunger and quenches thirst. I thought it not disagreeable. . . .

John Bell's reaction to the taste of buttered tea is understandable; most Westerners find it strange at first. His experience, however, was a pleasant one, because he encountered not only a typical Mongolian drink, but also the courteous hospitality that was (and still is) a central feature of Mongolian society.

John Bell, *A Journey from St. Petersburg to Pekin 1719–22*, edited by J. L. Stevenson (Edinburgh: Edinburgh University Press, 1966), p. 89; quoted in Reay Tannahill, *Food in History*, 2nd ed. (Harmondsworth, Middlesex: Penguin Books, 1988), p. 269.

of exchanging snuff established a cordial tone for whatever conversation might follow. In modern Mongolia, this practice has been discouraged by the socialist government as a "feudal custom," but it still may be found, especially in the countryside and among older people. Today, as in the past, hospitality and etiquette are regarded by most Mongols as an indispensable element of the pleasures of life.

Mongolia and the World Today

The Mongols, who once ruled much of the world, now play a very small role in international affairs. The Mongolian People's Republic is by no means a small nation, but it is dwarfed by its two giant neighbors, the Soviet Union and China. The country is about twice the size of Texas, but its entire population is smaller than that of the city of Houston. The land is rich in livestock, minerals, and rivers with hydroelectric potential, but Mongolia's gross national product—the total value of everything produced in the *entire* country in one year—is only $1.8 billion, about 1 percent of the annual budget *deficit* of the United States government in recent years.

Under these circumstances, Mongolia has been content to pursue a program of socialist development under the guidance and protection of the Soviet Union. It relies heavily on Soviet aid and, in return, has followed unquestioningly the lead of the Soviet Union in both domestic and international affairs. Only in very recent years has Mongolia begun

An idealized view of modern Mongolia: Poster depicting Mongols of all walks of life— traditionally dressed country folk, an urban bureaucrat, a military officer, a schoolgirl, and even a cosmonaut—walking together in Sükhe Baatar Square, Ulan Bator. Mongolia *magazine, No. 4, 73, 1983*

to emerge from the Soviet shadow to pursue more independent and nationalistic policies at home, and to cultivate wider diplomatic and trade contacts with the noncommunist world.

Domestic Policy

Mongolia's progress in nation building and modernization in the twentieth century has been impressive by any standard. In 1920, on the eve of the Mongolian Revolution, Mongolia was one of the poorest and most miserable countries in the world. Life expectancy and infant mortality were among the world's worst, and the population was declining. Much of the country's wealth was monopolized by a small aristocracy and by Buddhist temples that had grown lax and corrupt. Mongolia's commerce was almost entirely in the hands of Chinese merchants. The country had no railroads, no paved roads, and no motor vehicles. Mongolia seemed to be on the road to national extinction.

Today Mongolia remains a poor country, but is firmly in the ranks of the developing nations of the Third World. Medical care, life expectancy, and literacy are at levels comparable to those of other developing nations. A vigorous program of urbanization and industrialization has created modern cities, basic manufacturing industries, and national networks of transportation and communications. The development of state farms and textile mills has made the country at least partly independent of imported grain and cloth. Perhaps most important, a vigorous sense of national pride has replaced the downtrodden aspect of the Mongolia of seventy years ago.

Gandan Monastery, Ulan Bator. Traditionally one of Mongolia's most important religious centers, Gandan Monastery is today one of the few functioning monasteries in the secular, communist society of the Mongolian People's Republic.

Naturally, this rapid development has had its price. Lamaistic Buddhism has been virtually wiped out in the M.P.R., and with it important aspects of Mongolia's old national culture. In many other respects, the government has promoted and preserved traditional arts, sports, and folkways as a matter of preference and national pride, but elements of traditional culture and social life that the modern government regards as "feudal" have been suppressed. The ruling Mongolian People's Revolutionary Party has been a tightly disciplined and stern Communist party in the Stalinist mold; it has perhaps brought a degree of even-handed public administration to the masses, but at the cost of severe repression of broader democratic tendencies and of creative freedom among the country's artists and intellectuals. (For more on the Soviet background of modern Mongolian politics and culture, see *The Land and People of the Soviet Union.*)

Urban and industrial development has proceeded rapidly and with little regard for environmental effects. Ulan Bator and other industrial cities suffer from severe air and water pollution. Visitors to Mongolia are often shocked at the contrast between the magnificent natural beauty of the countryside and the harsh ugliness of industrial areas.

More than that, development for Mongolia has meant acceptance of Soviet domination. The Mongolian economy is dwarfed by that of the Soviet Union, which absorbs much of Mongolia's industrial and mining output and serves as its principal market for hides, furs, meat, and other animal products. The Soviet Union and its Eastern European economic partners supply Mongolia with virtually all of its imported high-technology and heavy manufactured goods.

"Leap Over the Stage of Capitalism." According to orthodox Marxist theory, prerevolutionary Mongolia was in a feudal stage of development; this billboard near Ulan Bator urges people to make the transition directly to socialism, without passing through a capitalist phase.

In very recent years, perhaps inspired by the new Soviet policies of *glasnost* and *perestroika*, Mongolia has begun cautiously to reexamine the degree to which it has relied on the Soviet Union. Mongolia, which once unquestioningly followed the lead of the U.S.S.R. in almost everything, recently has seemed more willing to assert its own unique national identity. In 1984, the old and infirm party chairman and premier, Yumjaagiyn Tsedenbal, was forced to retire. He was replaced by Jambyn Batmonkh (as party chairman) and Dumaagiyn Sodnom (as premier). The thirty years of rule under Tsedenbal are now referred to as a period of "stagnation," implicitly criticizing Tsedenbal's unswerving pro-Soviet policies. Moreover, Tsedenbal's predecessor, Marshal Choibalsan, now is openly criticized as a Stalinist dictator. In response to popular demonstrations, the government recently legalized opposition parties and removed statues of Stalin from public places in Ulan Bator.

These recent shifts in Mongolia's political climate are beginning to be reflected in various concrete changes. Although the Russian Cyrillic alphabet remains in official use for writing the Mongolian language, the old-style Mongol script is now also taught in schools. The government now encourages people to wear traditional Mongolian dress; until recently, urban workers had been urged to wear Western-style (more specifically, Russian-style) clothing. Plans have been announced to restore several historically significant Lamaist temples. The government has also made it clear that environmental laws will be more strictly enforced, and several high officials have been threatened with prosecution for having permitted violations of those laws. And perhaps most significantly, Genghis Khan is being restored to a position of greater prominence in official versions of Mongolian history. Although Genghis Khan never ceased to be a popular hero, the M.P.R. government under Tsedenbal downplayed his role out of deference to Soviet feelings—because Russians had long memories of the Mongol invasions of the thirteenth century! (In 1962 a number of intellectuals and officials were purged after they mounted a celebration of the eight hundredth anniversary of Genghis Khan's birth.)

Soviet policy toward Mongolia has also begun to change. Soviet party leader Mikhail Gorbachev has made it clear that the nations of the Soviet bloc must take greater responsibility for their own economic development and rely less heavily on Soviet support. For Mongolia, this means that Russian aid can no longer be counted on to compensate for the inefficiency of an outmoded, centrally planned economy; homegrown economic reform and restructuring will be essential. It seems likely that further important changes in Mongolian politics and society, and in the Soviet-Mongolian relationship, will occur—perhaps at an accelerating pace—in the last decade of the twentieth century.

International Affairs

During the first three decades after the establishment of the M.P.R., Mongolia's willingness to accept Soviet leadership served a key goal of Mongolian national policy: to resist the possibility of Chinese expansionist ambitions. Mongolia was incorporated into the Chinese empire in 1691, and Russian aid in Mongolia's modern revolution was seen as a means of achieving liberation from China. If the price of liberation was domination by the Soviet Union, that price was worth paying. The Mongols of the M.P.R. feel a strong sense of kinship with Mongols in China as well as in the Soviet Union and elsewhere in the world. The Mongols of China's Inner Mongolian Autonomous Region and Xinjiang Province exemplify, for their neighbors and kinsmen to the north, what might have happened to them. China's Mongols enjoy a certain amount of self-rule in local affairs, a significantly greater amount of religious freedom than the Mongols of the M.P.R., and their own commitment to the preservation of traditional Mongolian culture. But they are a minority people even within their own homeland in China; ethnic Chinese immigrants to the Inner Mongolian Autonomous Region now far outnumber Mongols there. The Mongolian People's Republic includes only about half of the traditional homeland of the Mongolian people, but it is the one place in the world that Mongols can truly call their own nation.

The People's Republic of China, established in 1949, renounced all Chinese claims to Outer Mongolia, and recognized the M.P.R. as a fraternal socialist state. Nevertheless, many Mongols remained unconvinced that China had abandoned its old ambition to dominate Mongolia. Moreover, the Republic of China, from its government in exile on Taiwan, continued to claim that Outer Mongolia was part of China. That claim was not meaningless, because the Republic of China retained the Chinese seat in the United Nations until 1969, and continued to be recognized as the legal government of China by the United States and many other Western nations for several years more.

During the 1950's, the Soviet Union and the People's Republic of China maintained friendly relations, and Soviet advisors played an important role in rebuilding China's war-torn economy. This Sino-Soviet friendship provided Mongolia with a sense of security, because China apparently accepted Soviet leadership of the Communist world and the dominant position of the U.S.S.R. in Mongolia. In 1958, however, China expelled its Soviet advisors, and Sino-Soviet relations became quite hostile; during the 1960's and early 1970's, there were a number of incidents of armed conflict along the border between China and the Soviet Union. Mongolia lined up firmly with the Soviet Union in opposition to China, and a buildup of Soviet troops near the Mongolian border with China began. By the mid-1960's, several hundred thousand Soviet troops were stationed in Mongolia, and those troop levels were maintained for the next twenty years.

Throughout this period, Mongolia remained isolated from international affairs apart from its relations with the countries of the Soviet bloc. For a long time the international isolation of Mongolia was enforced in part by the hostility of the United States. After World War II the United States opposed the admission of Mongolia to the United Nations, on the one hand arguing that Mongolia was simply a satellite of the Soviet Union, rather than a true nation, and on the other hand upholding the claim of the Republic of China (Taiwan) that Mongolia was part of Chinese territory. American opposition to Mongolia softened under the Kennedy administration, and the Mongolian People's Republic was admitted to the U.N. on October 27, 1961.

Mongolia's real emergence into the wider world of international affairs did not begin, however, until the mid-1980's. One element of Soviet Premier Gorbachev's reform policies was to cultivate more friendly relations with the People's Republic of China. Throughout the 1980's, Sino-Soviet relations became more cordial. This not only reduced border tensions between China and the Soviet Union, but also gave Mongolia a renewed sense of security in its relations with China.

These events, together with the reform policies pursued in Mongolia by the post-Tsedenbal leadership, have had important consequences for the military situation along the Mongolian-Chinese border. In 1989, Mongolia announced that it would reduce its armed forces by over 50 percent, from 25,000 troops to twelve thousand. Along with this reduction in military personnel, much military equipment will be turned over to civilian uses or put into mothballs. What is more important, the Soviet Union announced in 1989 that it intended to reduce its military presence in Mongolia by 75 percent. This very visible relaxation of Soviet military domination should please Mongolian nationalists, although it will also involve the loss of one significant source of funds from the Soviet Union.

The forced retirement of Tsedenbal in 1984 signaled a turn toward greater openness to participation in international affairs well beyond the immediate borders of the M.P.R. Soon after the new Mongolian leadership took office, negotiations were begun with the United States (with Soviet encouragement) to exchange diplomatic recognition. The negotiations succeeded; the United States and Mongolia established diplomatic relations on January 27, 1987.

U.S. Secretary of State George Shultz and Mongolian Ambassador to the United Nations G. Nyamdoo signing documents establishing mutual diplomatic relations between the two countries, in Washington, D.C., January 1987. U.S. State Department Photo

Wider diplomatic contacts have been accompanied by wider trade relations. A factory built with Japanese investment has been exporting cashmere cloth from Mongolia for several years. Mongolian shoes, woolen carpets, and other light manufactured goods are finding their way onto the world market, and Mongolian vodka is now being imported into the United States. The Soviet Union remains both politically and geographically the principal customer for Mongolia's exports, but trade

The Choephel-Ling Mongolian Buddhist Temple, Howell Township, New Jersey. America's small community of Kalmuk Mongols continues to uphold the traditional Mongolian faith in Lamaistic Buddhism, under the leadership of the Dalai Lama of Tibet. The establishment of diplomatic relations between Mongolia and the United States has special meaning for Mongolian Americans, who have been cut off from their ancestral homeland for generations. Photo by Anna Kelden, 1984

The Soyombo

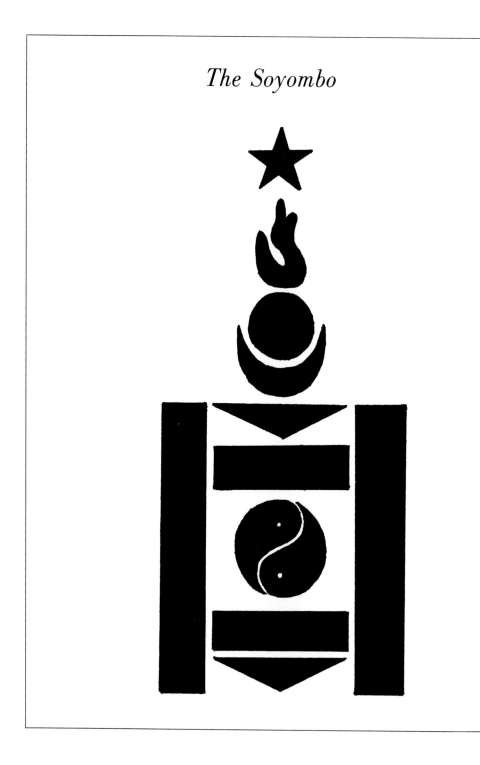

The *soyombo* (or *soyemba*) is the national emblem of Mongolia. Its origins are closely associated with Lamaism, and the various elements of the design were regarded as having mystical meanings. Individually, parts of the design also may be related to brands of ownership placed on horses and cattle.

The star at the top of the modern *soyombo* is a recent addition to the traditional symbol; it represents socialist revolution. Below that, a fire symbol has multiple significance. It represents revival and growth, and also the family hearth and the continuity of the people. The fire has three tongues of flame, symbolizing past, present, and future. Below the fire are symbols of the sun and moon, links to the pre-Buddhist nature religion of the Mongols.

In ancient Mongolian symbolism, an arrow or spear pointing to the ground meant death. In the *soyombo*, two downward-pointing triangles signify death to the enemies of the Mongols. Two horizontal rectangles represent honesty and fairness between rulers and the people.

Set between the two horizontal rectangles is the Chinese sign of yin and yang, representing dark and light, female and male, cold and hot—the unity of all opposites in the cosmos. In Mongolian symbolism, the figures in the yin-yang circle represent two fish which, because fish never close their eyes, signify reason and wisdom.

The two vertical rectangles represent a fortress, recalling the old Mongolian proverb "The friendship of two men is stronger than stone walls." The symbol of the fortress signifies that the unity of the Mongol people is the foundation of the nation's strength.

The *soyombo* was adopted as the official symbol of the Mongolian People's Republic by the first People's Great Khural in 1924. A golden *soyombo* is emblazoned on the left panel of Mongolia's blue-and-red national flag.

with China is also increasing—another reflection of the easing of tensions in Sino-Soviet relations. Mongolia remains a small, poor, and isolated country, but it is now definitely part of the world community.

The establishment of relations between the United States and the Mongolian People's Republic was little noticed by most Americans, for whom Mongolia remains remote and unimportant. But the event was celebrated in New York and Washington by gatherings of Americans of Mongolian descent from all over the eastern United States. For them the establishment of diplomatic ties between the two countries was a public recognition that the once great and still proud nation of Mongolia has a genuine role to play in the modern world.

Bibliography

Reference Works and Broad Topical Studies

The Cambridge History of China. 14 Vols. Cambridge, England: Cambridge University Press, 1978–.

A comprehensive history of China from about 250 B.C. to the mid-twentieth century, with detailed information on China's relations with Mongolia and Central Asia.

The Encyclopedia of Asian History. 4 Vols. New York: Charles Scribner's Sons, 1987.

An excellent reference work, covering all of Asia. Prepared under the auspices of The Asia Society.

Sechin Jagchid and Paul Hyer. *Mongolia's Culture and Society.* Boulder, Colo.: Westview Press, 1979.

The best comprehensive study of Mongolia in English.

Sechin Jagchid. *Essays in Mongolian Studies.* Provo, Utah: Brigham Young University Press, 1988.

Twenty-two essays on various aspects of Mongolian history, by one of this country's foremost authorities.

Mongolian Studies: Journal of the Mongolia Society.

The most important periodical for scholarly studies of Mongolia in English. Published annually by The Mongolia Society, c/o Department of Uralic and Altaic Studies, Indiana University, Bloomington, Ind. 47405.

Bibliography of Asian Studies. Ann Arbor, Mich.: Association for Asian Studies, annual.

The best source for recent publications on Mongolia and all of Asia.

Contemporary Affairs

Alan J. Sanders. *Mongolia: Politics, Economics, and Society.* (Marxist Regimes Series.) Boulder, Colo. Lynne Rienner, 1987.

An informative handbook on modern Mongolia.

Asian Yearbook. Hong Kong: Far Eastern Economic Review, annual.

Brief country-by-country surveys of the year under review, with emphasis on political events and economics.

Statistical Yearbook for Asia and the Pacific. New York: United Nations Publications, annual.

Country-by-country statistics on agricultural and industrial production, etc.

Mongolia. Ulan Bator: M.P.R. State Committee for Information, Radio, and Television, bi-monthly.

An illustrated bi-monthly magazine giving information on contempory Mongolia from the official point of view of the Mongolian government.

Nonprint Resources

"Music from Mongolia." Audio tape of a live performance at The Asia Society, New York, October 7, 1987. Available from the Department of Performances, Films, and Lectures, The Asia Society, 725 Park Avenue, New York, N.Y. 10021.

One of the best recordings available of traditional Mongolian music. Consult the same source for information on other recordings, videotapes, etc.

"Depending on Heaven: The Grasslands." 16 mm./VHS. First Run/Icarus Films, 200 Park Avenue South, New York, N.Y. 10003.

Documentary film (28 minutes) about a Mongolian herding family in the Inner Mongolian Autonomous Region of the People's Republic of China.

The Mongolia Society, c/o Department of Uralic and Altaic Studies, Indiana University, Bloomington, Ind. 47405.

The Mongolia Society is a good source for current information on Mongolian films, performances, and exhibitions in North America.

Permanent Mission of the Mongolian People's Republic to the United Nations, 6 East 77th Street, New York, N.Y. 10021.

Handles U.S.-Mongolian diplomatic relations pending establishment of a Mongolian Embassy in Washington. Distributes pamphlets and other literature (depending on availability) on contemporary Mongolia.

American Museum of Natural History, West 81st Street and Central Park West, New York, N.Y. 10024.

The Hall of Asian Peoples contains one of the best American ethnographic collections on Mongolia.

Suggestions for Further Reading

Chapter I
Who Are the Mongols?

Denis Sinor. *What Is Inner Asia?* Bloomington, Ind.: Indiana University Asian Studies
Research Institute, Teaching Aids for the Study of Inner Asia, I, 1975.
   A brief introduction to inner Asian geography and culture.

Chapter II
The Land

Stuart Legg. *The Heartland.* New York: Farrar, Straus, 1971.
   A very readable book on the history, geography, and culture of Central Asia.

Chapter III
Steppe Culture and the Rise of the Mongols

René Grousset. *The Empire of the Steppes: A History of Central Asia.* Transl. by Naomi Walford. New Brunswick, N.J.: Rutgers University Press, 1970.

> A standard general history of Central Asia.

Owen Lattimore. *Inner Asian Frontiers of China.* New York: American Geographical Society, 1940.

> This classic study of Inner Asia is particularly good on the origins of pastoral nomadism and the dynamics of steppe society.

Chapter IV
The Background of the Mongol Empire

Karl Jettmar. *Art of the Steppes.* Transl. by Ann E. Keep. London: Methuen, 1967.

> Steppe society in antiquity, viewed through its art.

Vladimir N. Basilov, ed. *Nomads of Eurasia.* Transl. by Mary Fleming Zirin. Seattle: University of Washington Press, 1989.

> Illustrated catalog of an exhibition of archaeological and ethnological materials, with twelve interpretive essays.

Chapter V
The Conquests of Genghis Khan

Michael Prawdin. *The Mongol Empire: Its Rise and Legacy*, 2nd ed. Transl. by Eden Paul and Cedar Paul. New York: The Free Press, 1967.

> A somewhat outdated but still very readable history of the Mongol Empire.

Peter Brent. *Genghis Khan: The Rise, Authority and Decline of Mongol Power.* New York: McGraw-Hill, 1976.

> A history of the Mongol Empire, very well illustrated.

Chapter VI
The Rise and Fall of the Mongol Empire

Morris Rossabi. *Khubilai Khan: His Life and Times.* Berkeley, Calif.: University of California Press, 1988.

A history of the Mongol Yuan Dynasty of China. Includes an excellent bibliography.

David Morgan. *The Mongols.* Oxford: Blackwell, 1986.
A history of the Mongol Empire, with emphasis on western Asia. Also includes an excellent bibliography.

Rashid al-Din. *The Successors of Genghis Khan.* Transl. by John Andrew Boyle. New York: Columbia University Press, 1971.
Contemporary account by a Persian historian who served at the court of the Ilkhans.

Chapter VII
A Nation in Decline

C. R. Bawden. *The Modern History of Mongolia.* New York: Praeger, 1968.
Covers the post-empire period, and emphasizes Mongolia's later dependence on the Soviet Union.

Chapter VIII
Mongolia Enters the Twentieth Century

History of the Mongolian People's Republic. Transl. by William A. Brown and Urgunge Onon. Cambridge, Mass.: Harvard University Press, 1976.
The most comprehensive book in English on modern Mongolia, but heavily propagandistic: history from the M.P.R. government's point of view.

Chapter IX
Culture and the Arts

Walter Hessig. *The Religions of Mongolia.* Transl. by Geoffrey Samuel. Berkeley, Calif.: University of California Press, 1980.
The best book on Mongolian religion.

Jambyn Badraa. "Characteristics of Mongolian Music and Dance." Transl. by B. Doljintseren *et al.* John S. Major, ed. New York: The Asia Society, Department of Performances, Films and Lectures Occasional Papers, 1987.
A good general introduction to Mongolian music and dance.

Paul Kahn. *The Secret History of the Mongols: The Origin of Chingis Khan.* Berkeley, Calif.: North Point Press, 1984.

A very readable adaptation of the classic work of Mongolian literature, based primarily on the scholarly translation by Francis Cleaves.

John R. Krueger, ed. *Mongolian Folktales, Stories, and Proverbs.* Bloomington, Ind.: Mongolia Society Occasional Papers No. 4, 1967.

Gives a good sense of traditional Mongolian folk literature.

O. Namnandorj and G. Amar. "National Sports." Ulan Bator: Mongolian Committee of Physical Culture and Sports, 1971.

Brief booklet describing the "three manly sports."

Chapter X
Daily Life

Silvio Micheli. *Mongolia: In Search of Marco Polo and Other Adventures.* Transl. by Bruce Penman. New York: Harcourt, Brace & World, 1967.

A lively and interesting account of an Italian journalist's travels throughout Mongolia in the early 1960s.

Lumír Jisl. *Mongolian Journey.* Transl. by Till Gottheiner. London: Artia/Batchworth Press, 1960.

A large-format book featuring excellent photographs of twentieth-century Mongolia.

Claude Arthaud and François Hébert-Stevens. *Mongolie: Dans les Steppes de Genghis Khan.* Paris: B. Arthaud, 1958.

Excellent photographs of daily life in modern Mongolia (text in French).

Chapter XI
Mongolia and the World Today

Owen Lattimore. *Nomads and Commissars: Mongolia Revisited.* New York: Oxford University Press, 1962.

Observations on contemporary Mongolia, by one of the West's foremost authorities.

————. *Nationalism and Revolution in Mongolia.* Leiden: E. J. Brill, 1955.

Lattimore sees widespread support in Mongolia for social and political revolution.

"Background Notes: Mongolia." Washington: U.S. Department of State, Bureau of Public Affairs, 1987.

Brief information on contemporary Mongolia, including a chronology of events since 1920.

Index

Numbers in *italics* refer to illustrations.

Babur, 102
Bactria, 53
Baghdad, 87, 93
Balkh, 72
Batmonkh, Jambyn, 176
Batu, 78–80, 82, 85–86, 89, 92
Bayan, 86, 90
Beijing, 33, 68, 70, 86, 90, 95
Benedict of Poland, 82
Berke, 89
biyelge (dance), 143
Black Sea, 102
blessings, 166
    See also yurol
Bogdo Gegen (Prince Bogdo), 117
Bogdo Genen Palace, 134, *136*, 137,
    140, *141*
Bolsheviks, 118–19
Budapest, 81
Buddhism, 11, 55, 84, 89, 109,
    122–23, *130*, 131–37, 159,
    172
    See also Lamaism
Büri, 80
Buriats, 13, 15, 107, 115–17
Burma, 86, 92, 94
Byzantine Empire, 81

camels, 4, 28, *29*, 30, 33, *44*, *114*,
    152
caravans, *10*, 33–34, *44*, 104, *114*,
    122
Carpini, Giovanni, 82
cashmere, 33, 39, *39*
Caspian Sea, 72, 75, 80
Cathay, 93, 95–97, 105
Catherine the Great, 101
Caucasus, 73, 89, 92, 113
Chagatai, 78–79, 89

Chagatid Khanate, 89, 91, 101–2
Chakhars, 116–17
Chakhars (tribe), 13, 15, 107, 109,
Champa, 93
chess, 150
Chiang Kai-shek, 120
children, 162
China, 12, 14–15, 17–18, 168, 170,
    177, 183
    Mongol conquest of, 67–69, 86, 90
    Republic of, 17, 117, 119, 124,
    126, 178–79
    People's Republic of, 18, 125–26,
    128, 177–79
Chinese frontier, dynamics of, 49,
    51–52, 104
Choibalsan (city), xv, 33
Choibalsan, Khorloin, 118–20,
    122–23, 127, 176
Christianity, 84, 131
Circassians (tribe), 73
circus, 145, 156
cities and towns, 11, 18, 28, 151,
    154–56
climate, 19, 22, 24–25, 28, 152,
    154
clothing, 49, 161, 165–66, *167*,
    176
Coleridge, Samuel Taylor, 95
collectives, 27, 127
communications, 33–35, 123, 172
Communist Party, Soviet, 118
confederations, tribal, 48, 60, 102,
    107
contraception, 162
cooperatives, 28, 127, 152, 156
cosmonauts, 157
Crimea, 73, 101
Crusades, 82
Cyrillic alphabet, 14, 124, 176

ABOUT THE AUTHOR

John S. Major is a Senior Editor at the Book-of-the-Month Club. Since getting his doctorate in Asian Studies at Harvard, he has been a professor at Dartmouth College, a program director at the Asia Society, the leader of a trip through the Soviet Union, China, and Mongolia, and the author of The Land and People of China.